Learn to play golf
IN 10 EASY LESSONS

Learn to play golf
IN 10 EASY LESSONS

The simple route to a complete game

Neil Tappin

hamlyn

An Hachette UK Company
www.hachette.co.uk

First published in Great Britain in 2011 by
Hamlyn, a division of Octopus Publishing Group Ltd
Endeavour House
189 Shaftesbury Avenue
London
WC2H 8JY
www.octopusbooks.co.uk
www.octopusbooksusa.com

Distributed in the U.S. and Canada by Octopus Books USA:
c/o Hachette Book Group
237 Park Avenue
New York, NY 10017

ISBN 978-0-600-62167-6

A CIP catalogue record for this book is available from the British Library

Printed and bound in China

10 9 8 7 6 5 4 3 2 1

Contents

Introduction 6

Introduction

For nongolfers it can be hard to understand. "How can you fall in love with a game that can leave you feeling so miserable?" is a question that I am often asked by those nearest and dearest to me. Here, however, lies the essence of what makes golf so addictive. As the millions who play this game regularly know, there is nothing quite like hitting the perfect golf shot, and it only takes one moment of revelation to keep you coming back for more time and again. Whether you are Tiger Woods or you are picking up the game for the first time, golf's addictive nature is based on one simple reality—we all want to hit those perfect shots more often.

To play this game successfully, you will need three basic attributes: a smooth, fluid swing that provides both power and poise; a deft touch around the greens that allows you to make a good score; and a strong mind that will help you block out trouble and see positive results from any scenario. Indeed, it is this finely balanced set of requirements that makes golf unique. Becoming equally proficient in these three contrasting areas is the perpetual challenge that golfers seek to master.

The good news for those who are picking up the game for the first time is that you don't have to shoot low scores to enjoy the many benefits the game can offer. Our unique handicapping system means that a beginner can compete against a good low-handicap player with every possibility of coming out on top. You will also enjoy the exercise and companionship that makes sport such an important part of people's lives.

The handicapping system provides a tangible way to judge your improvement—as you reach a consistently better level of play, your handicap will come down, reflecting your success.

This book has been designed to arm you with all the knowledge you require to get a foothold in golf. From cementing the keys to a solid swing to developing a pressure-proof feel around the greens, the pages that follow are filled with simple and effective advice that is guaranteed to trigger crucial improvements. No matter what level you already play to, there is something relevant to your level.

So whether you are picking up the game for the first time or rededicating yourself in a bid to make a long-term improvement, the ten easy lessons that follow will provide invaluable guidance in all areas of the game. The journey ahead will be long and, at times, frustrating but you will soon be rewarded with the sense of achievement that only comes with a truly well played golf shot. So all that's left to say is sit back, read on, and enjoy the journey.

Right To play golf successfully you need three things: a good swing, a deft touch, and a strong mind.

Before you start

Before we study the technique, there are some crucial elements of the game that you need to understand. Lesson one focuses on all the factors that regular golfers take for granted but that you may not already know. From the local golf club and the Rules of the game to choosing equipment and the best way to get started, this chapter should give you everything you need to know.

The course

At the typical golf course, there is far more than just 18 holes. In fact, the first thing you will see upon arrival is usually the clubhouse. This is where you can change your shoes, buy golf equipment, and enjoy post- and prematch refreshments. It is also here that you will find the pro shop. The club pro is a good person to know. He or she will be able to offer you lessons, provide crucial equipment advice, and sell you important items—anything from a set of irons to a ball marker.

Golf courses themselves come in a range of different styles (see below for more details) but they are usually made up of between 9 and 36 holes. A round of golf is 18 holes and, within this, each individual hole has a par. Most layouts feature a range of par-3, par-4, and par-5 holes—this creates a varied, comprehensive test. Depending on the course, the total par for 18 holes usually ranges between 70 and 72. The number of shots that you regularly play the course above the par will come to represent your handicap.

Those wanting to play have two options. You can join your local club and benefit from the challenge and companionship of partaking in regular competitions or you can play a range of different courses, paying a single green fee each time you play. The option you choose should reflect your own personal circumstances.

Each hole has a number of elements to it. You start on the "teeing ground," a flat area with markers from where you hit your first shot. Most holes have a "fairway," an area of closely mown grass from where you will want to hit your second shot, unless you are playing a short par-3 hole and have managed to hit the green with your tee shot.

If you have missed the fairway, you might be in the "rough," the longer grass placed there to trap your ball, making it hard to make a clean strike. Rough varies in length, usually getting thicker the farther you are from the fairway.

You then reach the "green," the manicured and smooth area of very short grass with a hole cut into it. You should only use your putter on the green to avoid taking divots.

The green and fairway may have "bunkers" on them—sizable holes filled with sand, which are designed as traps to gather your ball and make life awkward. There may also be water in the form of streams, ponds, or lakes, and there are all kinds of penalties if you are unfortunate enough to send your ball swimming.

Left This is an example of a beautiful par three on a parkland course.

COURSES TO CHOOSE FROM

One of the things that makes golf unique is its many different playing surfaces. On any given day, golfers can choose between vastly different layouts that are designed to offer slightly differing challenges. Below is a list of the most common courses and the challenges they pose:

● **Parkland** Inland layouts, which are often lush with danger coming in the shape of trees and water hazards

● **Links** This term refers to the land that links the sea to the mainland. The challenge here comes in the form of mastering strong coastal winds, avoiding deep "pot" bunkers and thick rough, and striking the ball cleanly from hard and fast fairways

● **Heathland** On heathland courses, the fairways are often lined with heather and bracken

● **Resort** The courses that are attached to modern resorts usually present a thoroughly modern challenge. These are often long with huge bunkers, vast greens, and well-positioned water hazards.

The Rules

Every golf course will provide a unique selection of challenges. Covering the many possible situations that can arise is a relatively easy-to-understand Rules Book, which is compiled by the game's two ruling bodies, the USGA (the United States Golf Association) and the R&A (the Royal and Ancient Golf Club of St. Andrews). The ruling bodies also publish a Decisions Book, which goes into specific scenarios in more depth, and this is helpful when unusual events take place.

Before you head to the course for the first time it is worth buying a Rules Book. You will notice that there are 34 Rules divided into various subsections, appendices, and notes. You do not need to know every rule in depth (even those who play the game for a living often don't!), but it is worth developing a general understanding so you know how to proceed in most scenarios.

The Rules are what make golf such a respected game. Those who are caught cheating are often unable to get rid of the negative reputation that follows them. Indeed, the reason the Rules are so well observed is because golf is largely a self-policing sport. You will often be the only person who knows that you have incurred a penalty, and accepting the extra shots without giving in to the temptation to turn a blind eye is a responsibility that is not to be taken lightly. Understanding the Rules will also help you avoid making potentially costly rules-related mistakes.

Above Take the time to develop an understanding of the Rules.

Above Wait patiently and quietly for your partner or opponent to play.

Etiquette

This refers to the unwritten rules regarding when you should play and how you should act on the course to ensure that you don't disturb your playing partners or other golfers. For instance, it is bad etiquette to allow your shadow to be cast over the line of another player's putt. Here are some more factors to look out for:

JARGON BUSTING

How the ball lies The lie refers to how the ball sits on the grass or in sand. When you have a good lie, the ball will be sitting up, ready for a clean, crisp contact. When you have a bad lie, the ball will be sitting down, requiring a precise contact for success.

● Never walk across the line of another player's putt; your footprints cause their ball to be bumped off line

● Never make a noise while another golfer is playing. Keep perfectly still and do not stand directly behind them, whether you are on the green, fairway, or tee

● Play quickly—do not hold up the group behind and keep in touch with the group in front. You don't have to rush through the course, but be conscious of the golfers around you

● Repair divots and pitchmarks (marks made by your ball landing on the green) and rake bunkers after you have been in them

● Never leave your bag on a green or tee box. When on the green, it is best to leave bags near the next tee to save time

● If you hit your ball toward other golfers, always shout "Fore." Failure to do so is sure to induce an angry response.

Essential Rules

Many golfers know the key Rules without a detailed knowledge of every subsection and clause, and there are certain Rules you simply must know. Below are the basic Rules that come into play whenever you hit the course. It is wise to take some time to digest the information that follows, as failure to know these crucial Rules could cost you shots. Arm yourself with the knowledge of these essential Rules and you will be able to take to the course with confidence.

Your clubs

You are allowed to carry only 14 clubs. You may think that this is a simple rule to stick to but many players have a number of clubs from which they can choose before a competitive round (a squad of clubs, including extra wedges, hybrids, or perhaps even a 2-iron). If you discover that you have left an extra wedge in your bag by accident and are carrying 15 clubs, then in match play you will lose each hole played with the extra club. In stroke play, you will have to add two penalty strokes for each hole played with 15 clubs.

Honor

This refers to who should play first from the tee. The player who recorded the best score on the previous hole should go first; this is called the "honor." After you have teed off, it is the player farthest from the green or hole who should go first.

Provisional ball

Golf can be a time-consuming sport, especially if you fail to hit fairways. One time-saving measure introduced by the ruling bodies allows players to hit a second ball when they fear that their first may be lost. The second ball is called a "provisional" and only becomes the ball in play once it is decided that the first is lost or your five-minute looking time runs out. Before hitting the second ball, you must declare that you are playing a provisional.

Hazards

When playing from a hazard, albeit a bunker or the edge of a water hazard, you should not ground your club before hitting the shot. By touching the sand with your club before playing, you will pick up one penalty shot in both match play and stroke play.

Unplayable lie

If you find your ball in a position where it simply cannot be played, you will need to take a one-stroke penalty drop. For this, you have three options:

● Drop the ball two clubs' length away from where it lies and no nearer the hole

● Go back and play from where you hit the last shot

● Draw an imaginary line from the hole to your ball and extend it back beyond your ball—you can drop as far back as you like.

Water

If your ball makes its way into a water hazard, you have three options:

● Play it as it lies (without grounding your club); this is only possible in shallow water and even then can result in you getting extremely wet!

● Go back and play the last shot again. Watch out for the water!

● Drop the ball two clubs' length back on a line from where it entered the water. Lateral water hazards, marked by red stakes and usually along the side of a hole, allow you to drop on the other side of the water as long as you are no nearer the hole. When you land in the water, you incur a penalty of one stroke in both match play and stroke play.

Above If your ball goes in the water, you have three options. Make sure you choose the right one!

MARKING YOUR BALL

On the green, players are allowed to mark the position of their ball. This means you can remove your ball from the line of another player's putt. While you have the ball in your hand, you are free to clean it before replacing it.

Equipment

The equipment you choose will have a huge bearing on your success. If you are just starting out, select clubs with larger heads, which will offer maximum forgiveness. When your feel for the game improves and your ball striking becomes more consistent, then you might want to opt for a lineup that will help you optimize your feel and control. The driver, used to hit long distances, and the woods, of various weights and sizes, are the most exciting clubs in the bag.

JARGON BUSTING

Loft The angle the club sits at relative to the perpendicular and which determines the ball's flight.
Clubhead The part of the club used to strike the ball.
Shaft The part of the club that runs from the grip to the clubhead.

A TYPICAL BAG

CLUB	Description
DRIVER	Longest club in the bag, biggest head
3-WOOD	Big, bulky head; shorter shaft and more loft than a driver
5-WOOD	A smaller head than 3-wood; shorter shaft and more loft
HYBRID	The size of the head sits between fairway woods and long irons
IRONS 3–9	Thin metal heads with changing lofts— the higher the number of the iron, the more loft
PITCHING	Rounded and lofted iron
SAND WEDGE	Rounded iron with a flat bottom and lots of loft
LOB WEDGE	Similar to sand wedge but with yet more loft
PUTTER	Usually a shorter club without loft

Above Fairway woods, such as these, offer good distance from the fairway.

Left There are many different types of balls to choose from, so ask your local pro for guidance.

Balls

There are many different types of balls and good players will be able to tell the difference between a hard ball, which is designed to improve distance, and a softer one that offers high levels of feel. If you are at the start of your golfing journey, opt for a ball that is relatively hard and durable. Once you start improving, it is worth sampling softer options as these may help your touch around the greens.

Shafts

Getting the correct shafts for your swing is essential. This is something that your local professional will be able to help you with. The basic rule here is: The slower your swing, the more flexible your shaft should be to let you gain the maximum amount of clubhead speed and distance. If you are a fast swinger, stiffer shafts will offer greater levels of control.

Grips

Your only contact with the club is your grip, so it is important that grips are kept in good condition. Depending on how often they play, most golfers should change the grips on their clubs once every couple of years.

Drivers

Your driver will be the biggest club in your bag. At first you might find it daunting, but with the large head also come high levels of forgiveness. Drivers come in many different shapes and the general rule is: The more square the head, the more forgiving they are. If you are buying a driver, test a range of models and opt for something that offers a good blend of power and accuracy.

3-wood and 5-wood

These fairway woods are designed to be hit from short grass and also off the tee. They should give more control off the tee but offer good distance when playing from the fairway.

Irons

There are many different makes of irons to choose from but all offer two basic styles: blades, or shallow cavities, and deep cavity backs. Blades have smaller heads with thinner toplines and are designed to help the best ball strikers shape their shots and control their distances. Deeper cavity-backed irons have larger heads and thicker toplines—with more weight lower and deeper in the head, they help golfers find a higher flight. The general rule here is: The larger the head, the more forgiving they are.

Hybrids

These are designed to be hit from a variety of lies. Because they are more forgiving than long irons but more controllable than fairway woods, many players opt for hybrids instead.

Above A driver is used from the tee.

Above Fairway woods can be used from the tee or fairway.

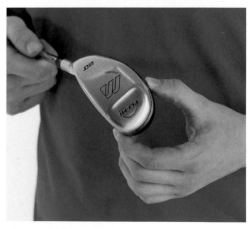

Above Hybrids are useful from a range of positions.

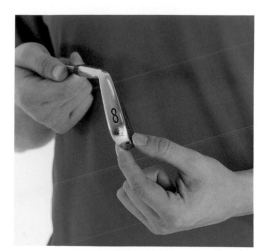

Above Your irons will make up the bulk of your clubs.

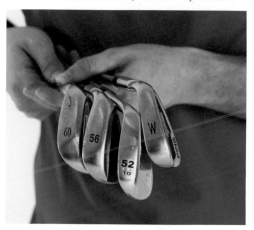

Above A number of wedges will help you score well.

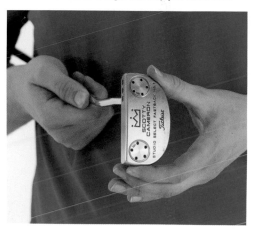

Above Putters are used on and around the green.

3-iron and 4-iron

These will be the most powerful irons in your bag. Notoriously hard to hit well, they tend to offer a lower flight than hybrids, and better players will enjoy the control.

5-iron, 6-iron, and 7-iron

These mid-irons are important scoring clubs. Striking these consistently well will help you find greens and set up good birdie and par opportunities.

8-iron and 9-iron

The short irons are also the most lofted. With these in hand, you should feel confident enough to aim at the flag.

Wedges

Selecting a sound lineup of wedges is essential for every golfer. A typical wedge lineup of 48° (pitching wedge), 52° (gap wedge), and 56° (sand wedge) enables players to hit certain key pitching yardages. However, your wedges are also used to chip and play bunker shots, so the key is to find the clubs that offer you the best feel and most control.

Putters

Putters come in all shapes and sizes. If you have a good natural feel on the greens, a smaller head will help you make the most of this strength. If you need help with your alignment or struggle on the greens, a larger head will improve your consistency. When buying a putter, seek advice on what would be the correct length of shaft for you. This is imperative as the best putters are able to address the ball with their eyes directly over it.

Different forms of golf

While the simple aim of the game of golf is always to get the ball in the hole in as few shots as possible, there are many different formats from which to choose. This is another unique aspect to golf, offering a variety of challenges. Every golfer has a preference for a particular version of the game and listed below are some of the most common forms. Read through the options and see just how much variety golf can offer.

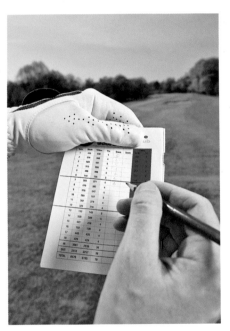

Above In stroke play, you mark down every score on the card.

Stroke play

Most professional tournaments, except the Ryder Cup and the occasional match play event, adopt this format. Simply, the person who takes the fewest number of shots wins. This can be from a single round to a four-round tournament.

Match play

When players go head-to-head, competing for individual holes instead of overall lowest score, the game is known as match play. Usually, players play as singles, comparing scores at the end of the hole, not the end of the round. If you win the first hole, you are one up; if you win the second, you are two up. However, as soon as your opponent starts winning holes back, this score gets shaved and you go back to one up, then all-square (level terms) and so on. You keep going until one player is more holes up than there remain holes to play, so if you are three up on the seventeenth tee, you have won three and two (three ahead with only two holes left). This format can also be played in two teams of two players.

Stableford

This is essentially stroke play but with one crucial difference—instead of marking the number of strokes you play on any particular hole, you score points. The points system is worked out by your net score (after the handicap is deducted) relative to the par of any particular hole. You will receive two points for a net par, one point for a net bogey, and no points for anything worse. For example, if you play off a handicap of 18, this means you get one extra shot in relation to par on every hole. By recording a five on a par-4, you will have scored a net par and in Stableford this is worth two points. In this format, a birdie is worth three points and a net eagle is worth five. If you play to your handicap for the round, your overall score will be 36 points.

Four-ball

When four golfers play their own ball in the round, they are playing a four-ball. Players will often go head-to-head in two teams of two with the best single score from each team on each hole counting.

Above Playing as a four offers many different competitive options.

Foursomes

Played again in two teams of two, foursomes forces players to hit alternate shots. For instance, you would hit your team ball off the first tee and your partner would hit the second shot, and so on. Players on each team take it in turns to hit off the tee.

Greensomes

A similar format to foursomes but instead of taking alternate shots from the tee, everyone drives, each pair selects the best drive, the other is picked up, and you play alternate shots from there until you hole out. Again, this may be used in a stroke play or match play format.

Scramble

This is a fun format where players usually head out in groups of four and play as one team. Every player hits off the first tee and the best shot is chosen, then everyone plays from there and so on. With four attempts at every shot, scramble scores tend to be very low.

How to get started

The tips and advice in this book will undoubtedly help you develop a technique and feel for the game, but becoming an expert golfer requires skill time and practice. If you are serious about reaching your potential, you should follow the guidelines below: head to the driving range, get lessons, take advice, and think about joining a club. Taking a sensible approach to improvement may lie at the heart of your longevity in the game.

Above A professional will help you develop the basic keys to good technique.

Head to the driving range

The first thing you should do is head to the driving range. Without the pressure of wanting to play well or not breaking any of the game's many Rules, the driving range is the perfect place to jump-start your enjoyment. Use the tips and drills in this book to build a solid fundamental technique. Once you have established these, you will make rapid improvements. To get the most from your practice time, it has to be fun, so going to the range with a friend and recording your improvement is always worthwhile.

Get lessons

Once you've started to enjoy the challenge of striking the ball, take a series of lessons from your local professional. He or she will help fine-tune your technique to ensure that bad habits do not creep in from the start. Building up a good relationship with a pro will be very beneficial as they can lend advice and support on a range of different golfing matters.

Take equipment advice

It is always a good idea to take equipment advice from a qualified PGA professional. They will ensure that you have the correct heads and shafts to complement your natural swing. It is important, however, that you test any equipment before you buy. The most important thing of all is to feel confident as you stand over the ball, and you are the only person who truly knows what feels comfortable.

Think about joining a club

You do not have to join a golf club, but after taking lessons and buying clubs this may be the fastest way to improve. By joining a club, you will meet other like-minded golfers, and the competition available may spur you on to improve. Golf clubs have regular competitions and the club secretary will also keep your handicap, giving you a "handicap certificate," which will allow you to take part in competitions away from your home club.

Below Finding the right equipment is essential to help you reach your potential.

The address position

It is often said that all mistakes in the swing can be traced back to faults in one position. The way you stand to the ball before you swing is the most important aspect of the game to get right. The next time you watch professional golf on television, take some time to look at the techniques shown. While there are plenty of unusual swings, they all have solid fundamental address positions. Learning this position well, so that you are comfortable, athletic, and ready to take the club back on the right path, is essential.

JARGON BUSTING

The address position
The way you stand to the ball before you swing.

WHY IS THE ADDRESS POSITION SO IMPORTANT?

Coaches all over the world stress the importance of a good address position because without it an effective swing can be found only by implementing various compensations. If you can nail down the five key elements, you will be free to make a simple, uncomplicated swing. From a good address position, you can turn back and through, finding a clean strike and powerful ball flight. So, if there is one position to practice over and again, it's the address.

A solid position

There are five elements to a solid address position. They are as follows:

• **Grip** Holding the club so your hands work together to keep the clubface on-line while also allowing for a fluid, powerful movement

• **Posture** The angle of your spine at address has a huge bearing on the overall consistency of your ball striking

• **Alignment** Standing square to your target not only gives you the best chance of hitting a straight ball but also allows you to take the club back on a good path

• **Stance** How your weight is positioned at address is another important aspect that is different for various shots

• **Ball position** Where the ball sits in comparison to your feet affects the angle that the club strikes the ball. Getting this right lies at the heart of sweet striking and piercing ball flights.

Right The basics are the most important aspect of a good game.

The grip

The way in which you hold the club has a huge bearing on the accuracy and consistency of your shots. The advice that follows will teach you how to achieve the correct grip and ensure your hands work together, generating both power and control. This will feel strange at first but the importance of the right grip cannot be emphasized enough. A good grip is one of those key elements that you need to master.

The correct grip

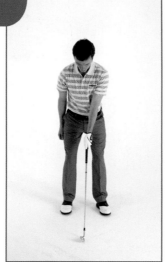

1 Start by placing your left hand on the club. The top half of the grip should run from the middle of your index finger to the base of your little finger. Once you are happy that the club is in this position, simply wrap the fingers of your left hand around the grip.

2 Move your left hand down, so the club sits on the ground. Your thumb should point straight down the grip, pointing at the clubhead, and you should be able to see the top two knuckles of your left hand.

3 Now place your right hand on the club, so the palm of your right hand sits on your left thumb. Like your left-hand grip, the club should run from the base of your little finger to the middle of your index finger. There are two options relating to the way in which your hands link together here (see page 26 for more details).

Right The "V" of your right hand should point to your right shoulder.

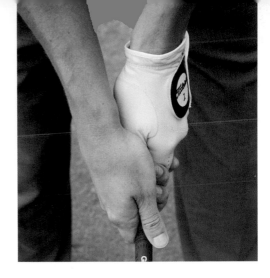

THINK...
Your left thumb points straight down the club; the "V" of your right hand points at your right shoulder.

4 **Now place the club on the ground again and take a look at your hands. The "V" created between your right thumb and index finger should point toward your right shoulder blade.**

Feeling comfortable

At first, this grip will feel strange, but do not be put off by this. You need to persevere with setting the right grip because the way your hands sit on the club directly affects how the clubhead works through the swing. If your hands are in a bad position, the clubface will either be open or closed through impact, causing destructively wayward shots. As you practice, run through the step-by-step guide before hitting each shot. This might seem somewhat excessive, but by the end of your practice routine, you will start to feel comfortable with your hands in this position. Before long, it will feel strange to grip the club in any other way and you will have nailed down one of the most important elements of a solid technique.

Grip pressure

The golf swing should be a powerful, athletic movement and as you prepare for this it might seem correct to grip the club tightly. However, if you choke the grip, tension will build in your forearms, restricting the fluid movement that allows you to create good clubhead speed through impact. Think of a scale between one and ten in which ten is the tightest you can hold the club and one is the softest. Look to hold the club at three on this scale. Your grip should be strong enough to control the club through the swing but soft enough to make a fluid, tension-free movement.

Linking your hands

To hit consistently straight shots, your hands need to work together and for this they must be linked. There are two options. You can choose the most common—the Vardon grip (named after the first player to use it, five-times Open Champion Harry Vardon)—or you can adopt an interlocking grip. Try both and go for the one that feels most comfortable.

Vardon grip The little finger of the right hand overlaps the index finger of the left.

Interlocking grip The little finger of the right hand interlocks with the index finger of the left.

Checking your grip

Every golfer, no matter what standard, should take time to check their grip. There are two common mistakes that can slip into your setup without you noticing. So here are the two most common grip-related faults. Check that these don't creep into your game.

Common errors

THINK...

Link your right and left hands together. Check your grip regularly, ensuring that it is neither weak nor strong.

STRONG GRIP

A strong grip has a tendency to close the clubface through impact, causing a hook (the ball curls to the left of target). With a strong grip, when you look down at your hands at address, the "V" between the thumb and index finger of your right hand will point to the right of your right shoulder. You will also be able to see three knuckles on your left hand.

WEAK GRIP

This causes the clubface to open through impact, creating a slice (the ball curves to the right of target) that will cost you both accuracy and yards. With a weak grip, the "V" will point toward your chin or even your left shoulder and you will only see one knuckle at address.

PRACTICE DRILL

To achieve a neutral grip, practice doing the following:

Take your normal address position and let your hands hang naturally down without a club. Place your hands together, so the tips of your fingers point at the ball.

Now mimic your normal swing but stop your hands just as you reach impact. The back of your left hand should point directly at the target.

Posture

Setting the perfect posture is far more important than you might think. With your spine at the right angle, your hands can hang down naturally, allowing you to make a simple back and through turn to find a clean, consistent strike. Becoming comfortable in the right position is imperative. Here's how to set the perfect posture. Take your time to follow the step-by-step instructions on this page and good ball striking will follow.

Setting your spine angle

1 **Start by standing upright.** Take your normal grip and hold the club out in front of you. Ensure that your back is straight and that your feet are shoulders' width apart.

2 **Keeping your hands out in** front of you, bend at the hips, lowering your upper body over the ball. Do not let your spine bend here. At first, this might feel more comfortable but it will affect the quality of the turn you make during the backswing.

3 **Now flex your knees. In the** ideal position, there should be around a hand's width between your thigh and the butt end of the club, and your knees should be above the laces of your shoes.

Mirror drills

A mirror is always useful to highlight to you the flaws in your address position. At most driving ranges, you'll find a mirror behind some of the bays. These are incredibly useful when it comes to checking your address position. In particular, by turning your head at setup you will be able to view the quality of your posture. It is important, however, that you do not lift your head when you turn to look in the mirror.

Above Take a look at your posture at address in the mirror.

Common errors

> ### THINK...
> Keep your back straight, flex your knees, and let your hands hang down naturally.

TOO RIGID

Never forget that the golf swing is an athletic movement, and in the address position you need to feel like an athlete in the blocks, ready to spring into action. Your knees must remain flexed, as much of the power you generate during the swing comes from your leg action.

LAZY POSTURE

Take a look at the position above. This, too, lacks the athleticism required, because when you are hunched over the ball, you will find it almost impossible to make a good turn.

POSTURE

Alignment

Alignment is crucial for two reasons. The first is obvious: Without aiming in the right direction, it is very difficult to hit accurate shots. The second reason is perhaps even more important. If your alignment is wayward, you will start to make compensations in your swing. The usual result is that the path of the swing gets knocked off-line, causing too much sidespin at impact. Take a few minutes to check your alignment every time you practice.

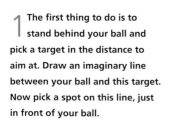

Setting up straight

1 The first thing to do is to stand behind your ball and pick a target in the distance to aim at. Draw an imaginary line between your ball and this target. Now pick a spot on this line, just in front of your ball.

2 Without setting your stance, aim the clubface directly at the spot in front of you. The clubface will be aiming directly at the target.

3 Now set your stance. Ensure that your feet, hips, and shoulders are all square to your ball-to-target line. Now you are perfectly aligned.

Using two clubs, point one directly at the target and the other parallel to this. The club pointing at the target is your reference for the position of the clubface. The club parallel to that will help you set your feet, hips, and shoulders square to your ball-to-target line. This is an incredibly simple yet effective way to practice.

THINK...

Point the clubface at the target and set your feet square to the ball-to-target line.

Below Your feet should be parallel to your ball-to-target line.

JARGON BUSTING

Ball-to-target line or target line The imaginary line between your ball and your target.

Square This can refer to the clubface or to your body. Your clubface is square if it is aimed directly at the ball-to-target line. Your body is square when your shoulders, knees, and toes are all aligned parallel to the ball-to-target line.

Open The clubface or body aims left of the target line.

Closed or shut The clubface or body aims right of the target line.

ALIGNMENT

Ball position

The next position to look at is where the ball sits in relation to your feet at address. The correct ball position allows you to find the ideal angle of attack—and this angle is different for different clubs. By setting the correct ball position, you will be able to find the optimum flight for any particular club. Once you feel confident with your swing and ball striking, you will be able to manipulate this position to take advantage when the wind starts to blow or when your ball sits in a difficult lie.

How to set the right ball position

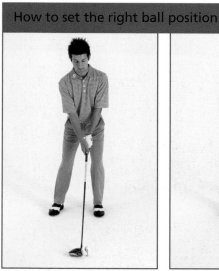

DRIVER
With a driver in hand, the ball should sit opposite your left heel. This allows you to strike the ball on the upswing, creating a shallow angle of attack for an optimum ball flight that delivers impressive carry through the air.

MID-IRON
With a mid-iron, set the ball in the middle of your stance. With the ball farther back than for a driver, a more descending angle of attack will ensure that you catch the ball before the turf.

SHORT IRON
Move the ball fractionally farther back in your stance with your shorter clubs. Again, this will help you find the clean strike you are after while offering good backspin to control distance.

CHECKING YOUR BALL POSITION

As when checking your alignment, you can also use clubs to check your ball position. First, lay two clubs down to check your alignment and then, depending on whether you are playing a driver or an iron, lay another shaft down perpendicular to the other two between your feet and the ball. This shaft will illustrate exactly where the ball is sitting in relation to your stance.

THINK...
Ball forward and weight on the right side when hitting your woods; ball in the middle of the stance and weight split evenly when hitting your irons.

Weight distribution

Weight distribution and ball position go hand in hand. Like your ball position, the way in which your weight sits at address affects the angle at which the club attacks the ball. With a driver or fairway wood in hand, you should have around 60 percent of your weight on your right side. This will shallow out your angle of attack, ensuring that you are behind the ball at impact, delivering a strong flight with impressive carry.

As you move into your mid- and short irons, your weight should be split evenly between both feet. This creates the steeper angle of attack that you need for a clean, crisp contact.

Right Move your weight toward the target through the downswing and forget the loft of the club.

Setting your stance

The way in which you take your stance will have a huge bearing on the shot that follows. That is why you should never rush into your address position but, instead, follow a simple routine that gets you into the perfect position every time. The step-by-step guide that follows will help you stand perfectly square to the target line with the ball in the ideal position in relation to your feet, enhancing both the quality and accuracy of your ball striking.

The perfect stance

1 **Start by aiming the clubface at the target.**

2 **Take your normal posture but set your feet next to each other. The line between your heels should be directly opposite the ball. Ensure that your feet, hips, and shoulders are square to your ball-to-target line.**

3 **Move your feet into position. The way you do this depends on which club you are hitting. With a driver, move your right foot to the right until your feet are the perfect width apart. This is the ideal position from which to hit a driver. If you are hitting an iron, move both feet away from each other by a couple of inches.**

Stance width

When setting the width of your stance there is another simple rule to follow. With your irons in hand, your feet should be shoulders' width apart. With a driver, however, they should be slightly farther apart. This creates a more stable hitting platform to make a powerful turn. With the shorter clubs, you may want to allow your stance to become a fraction narrower than shoulders' width apart. When playing in strong winds, widen your stance a fraction more than usual. This will give some crucial extra stability to your swing.

Below With a driver, set a wide stance and move the ball forward.

CHECKING YOUR STANCE

You can check the width of your stance by hanging two clubs down from your shoulders as shown. This gives you a clear reference to where your feet should be.

Troubleshooting

Whether you have a weak slice, a destructive hook, or catch all your iron shots fat, consistent mistakes can almost always be traced back to simple errors in the address position. The good news is that these errors are usually relatively simple to rectify as long as you know what to look out for. Below are some of the most common errors made in the address position. Take a look at these positions and guard against them creeping into your game.

Ball too far back

An error that often creeps in, especially if you have been playing golf in windy conditions, is to let your ball position move too far back in your stance. This either causes thin strikes or creates excess backspin, which will balloon the ball up into the air. Check your address position in a mirror from square on and you will soon see the error.

Above If the ball is too far back, your angle of attack will be too steep.

JARGON BUSTING

Thin When you strike the equator of the ball with the leading edge of the club.
Fat When you strike the grass before the ball, causing a weak strike that comes up short.

Opening your body

As you address the ball and look down, everything seems fine. The clubface is pointing at the target and your feet are square to your ball-to-target line. However, there is often a tendency to let the upper body open up, pointing left. This will cause you to cut across the ball at impact, slicing it to the right. Again, you can check by aiming directly at a mirror to see if your body is square—remember to look at your shoulders and hips as well as your feet.

Right If your body is open to your target line, a wayward slice is the likely outcome.

Right Some players have a tendency to open their upper body at address.

Far right If you stand too far back from the ball, your address position will be too rigid.

Aiming left

For many amateur golfers, the most common mistake is to hit a slice. As you see the ball drift right, it seems to make sense to aim farther left to compensate. This, however, will accentuate the problem. By aiming left, you will cut across the ball even more, creating destructive left-to-right spin at impact.

Not letting your arms hang naturally down

Another common error is to push your arms away from your body at address. If the ball sits too far from your body, finding a clean strike is almost impossible. Use the step-by-step guide on page 32 to find a more comfortable, athletic position.

Checklist

You should now have learned all the keys that are necessary to make a technically sound swing. The address position is essential, so use this checklist whenever you practice to ensure that no simple errors have crept in.

Grip

Find a neutral grip where the back of your left hand points at the target. You should see two knuckles in your left hand as you look down at address and the "V" between your right thumb and index finger should be pointing to your right shoulder. Keep your hands relaxed to find a fluid, rhythmical swing.

Posture

Make sure your back is straight, that you bend from the hips, and that your knees have a good amount of flex at address. Your hands should hang naturally down, so the butt end of the club sits a hand's width away from your thigh.

Alignment

Aim your clubface at the target and set your feet, hips, and shoulders square to your ball-to-target line. Place clubs on the ground to check that your angles are correct.

Ball position

Place the ball just inside your left heel when hitting a driver, move the ball into the middle of your stance for a mid-iron, and set it a fraction farther back for a short iron. Your weight should be split evenly between your feet when hitting your irons, with slightly more on your right side when hitting a driver.

Stance

Your feet should be shoulders' width apart when hitting with your irons and slightly wider when you hit with your woods.

Checking errors

Use mirrors either in your home or at the driving range to check these key static positions. Look at your grip, posture, alignment, and ball position to make sure that your fundamentals are rock solid.

The swing

When it comes to the swing, there are two basic things you need to control: the path of the club and the angle of the clubface. These are the two factors that affect the direction of the ball flight. So lesson three is devoted to all the areas that can affect these two crucial factors.

It is the path of the swing that is responsible for creating sidespin at impact. If the club travels from outside the target line to inside through impact, you will impart left-to-right spin on the ball with a fade or slice being the most likely outcome. Conversely, if the club travels inside to outside the target line, which is what we will try to help you achieve, you will create right-to-left spin at impact. Ensuring that the angle the club travels on through the hitting area is not too severe is the key to hitting reliably accurate shots.

Establishing the perfect swing, however, is meaningless if the clubface does not point in the right direction at impact. The good news is that if you've mastered a neutral grip, there is no reason why the club should not be square at impact. Over the following pages, we will provide all the keys necessary to master these two crucial elements.

POWER AND RHYTHM
The other important factors covered in this section are power and rhythm. Thankfully, these two go hand in hand. If you make an effective upper body turn, releasing the club powerfully through the ball, you will find good natural distance. If these moves are rhythmical, creating a steady build up of pace through the swing, you will add accuracy to your power.

Opposite Swing the club on a good path with power and accuracy and your scores are guaranteed to improve.

The takeaway

The first move you make is crucial. This is when you set the rhythm and path of the swing. Keeping this movement simple without any unnecessary extra movements is the key to success. The step-by-step guide that follows will help you set a passive but rhythmical takeaway. Get the takeaway right and you'll find both power and accuracy with ease; however, get it wrong and simple errors will creep in.

Rhythm and timing

The question is often asked, "How do the best players in the world hit the ball so far without looking as if they hit it hard?" The answer is rhythm. A steady build up of pace will help you keep your body movement under control and find power when you need it most, through impact.

The takeaway

1 The first movement is simple. Keep your wrists solid and move the club directly away from the target line. Take the club back at a smooth pace and don't let your posture or knee flex change.

2 The next move is to hinge your wrists. If the grip you set at address is correct, the toe of the club should point to the sky in the position above. Place a club on the ground between your feet and the ball as shown. Halfway back, the shaft of your iron should be parallel to the club on the ground.

THINK...
Take the club back on the ball-to-target line without disrupting your posture.

Left A good takeaway will ensure you get into a technically sound position at the top of the backswing

Leg action

As you take the club back, it is important that your lower body remains passive. One of the biggest mistakes you can make is to ruin the effect of a solid address position by letting your knees flex or straighten, or letting your hips sway as you take the club back. So keep your legs passive and prepare for a full effective turn.

Common errors

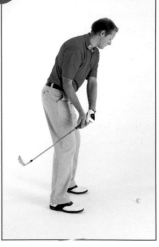

OUTSIDE THE LINE

If you take the club away outside the ball-to-target line (away from your body), you'll be preparing yourself to hit a slice. The only way to make a decent contact is to cut across the ball through impact, creating left-to-right spin.

INSIDE THE LINE

The opposite applies if you take the club away on the inside (toward your body). This simple mistake will cause you to hit a hard draw, or a hook. Remember that you can use a mirror at the driving range to check your takeaway.

Wrist hinge

As we have already touched on, your wrist hinge needs to come at the right time to keep the clubhead working on a good line. If correct, it will also help you reap all the benefits of making a full, athletic turn. Spend 10 minutes learning the right wrist hinge and your power and accuracy are guaranteed to improve. Read the guidelines that follow for how to achieve a perfect hinge, and try to build these into your technique.

Keep it compact

A long swing is not necessarily a powerful swing. Many of the world's longest hitters actually have relatively compact movements. It is the power of your rotation and how your wrists hinge and release that are the real keys to creating power. So remember that you can retain power and control by making a compact swing. More often than not, you will actually lose power by swinging too far back.

A perfect hinge

1 Having made a passive initial takeaway, you should hinge your wrists, so the toe of the club points at the sky. The angle between your arms and the shaft should stay the same from here to the top of the backswing.

2 As you move toward the top of your backswing, keep your left arm straight and your wrists solid. This is an incredibly simple and powerful position that will allow you to create good clubhead speed through impact.

Common errors

THINK...
Hinge your wrists as you take the club back, then maintain this angle to the top of the backswing.

INSIDE OR OUTSIDE THE LINE
Make sure that when you set your wrists, the club is not thrown off line. As in the initial takeaway, if the club moves inside or outside the ball-to-target line, you will be forced to create unnecessary sidespin through impact.

TOO MUCH HINGE
One mistake that players often make, believing it will offer extra power, is to employ too much wrist hinge at the top of the backswing. The position here lacks any power because it requires a flick of the wrists as opposed to a powerful turn of the body to reach impact.

JARGON BUSTING

Clubhead speed How fast your clubhead travels as you hit the ball. The faster it travels, the farther the ball flies.
Overswing When the club is swung too far in the backswing, causing a loss of power.

Left Remember not to upset your low, passive takeaway before hinging your wrists.

WRIST HINGE

Rotation

The rotation of your body lies at the heart of hitting powerful golf shots. The resistance created between your upper and lower body at the top of the backswing creates tension. This stored energy is then released through the downswing, providing impressive clubhead speed. At the top of your backswing, you should feel like a coiled spring, ready to unwind through the downswing. This is where the golf swing requires athleticism and poise. Here's how to do it.

Hip turn

As your upper body rotates 90 degrees, so that your back faces the target, your hips should rotate just 45 degrees. It is the difference between the angles here that creates the powerful coil at the top of the backswing. To illustrate just how powerful this position is, swing to the top and hold your position. If you have made a good turn, with your hips rotating only 45 degrees, you should find this position really hard to hold.

Rotation practice drill

1 **Take your normal set-up position and hold a shaft across your shoulders. It is important to make sure that your posture is correct as this has a huge bearing on the power of your turn.**

2 **Now rotate your upper body, so that your back faces the target. If you have made a full, athletic turn, the butt end of the club will point just to the right of the ball. Not every golfer has the same level of flexibility. If you can't quite turn your back to face the target, don't worry—just turn as far as you can.**

Left Be careful to maintain the posture you set at address to the top of your backswing.

POSTURE CHECK

It is worth pointing out at this stage that the posture you were so careful to set at address should remain the same to the top of the backswing and then through to impact. As their upper body rotates, some players allow their head to rise or dip. Be careful to guard against this; any simple errors here will lead to poor-quality contacts.

THINK...

Make a full upper body turn, rotate your hips 45 degrees, and maintain the spine angle you set at address.

Rotation errors

Not every golfer has the natural flexibility to make a full, athletic turn. Even if you can't turn your body fully to the target, there are certain crucial errors that you simply must guard against. Take a good look at the mistakes featured on these pages and make sure they do not creep into your game. A simple and effective turn coupled with a good weight shift lie at the heart of a powerful swing that is so crucial in the modern game.

Swaying

Later in this chapter, we will look specifically at how you should use your weight during the swing. As you move back, it is important that your weight sets naturally onto your right side. However, you must not sway as you take the club away. This is one of those unnecessary movements that will require compensations through the downswing.

Not turning

This fault is often made by players who are desperate to hit a straight shot. As you can see, the arms have swung to the top but the back has hardly rotated. This makes it incredibly hard to make a coordinated move through the downswing, usually resulting in a wayward shot. To prevent this, simply concentrate on turning your back to face the target.

Right Don't sway into the top of the backswing as this makes a good strike hard to find.

PRACTICE DRILL

Place a club on the ground between your feet and perpendicular to the ball. Now move to the top of your backswing. Make sure that your head does not move too far to the right of the club. A small amount of lateral head movement is fine, but this drill will highlight if your upper body is swaying too much.

THINK...

Keep your body centered and make a full upper body turn.

Reverse pivot

This is an incredibly common mistake born from a desire to help the ball into the air. With your weight on the right side at the top, your weight will have no option but to move away from the target through the downswing to get the ball airborne. Again, concentrate on keeping your sternum over the ball through the backswing and trust the loft of the club to get the ball up and away.

JARGON BUSTING

Reverse pivot When your weight moves in the wrong direction through the swing. At the top, your weight will be on your left side; and through impact it is on your right side.

Right Make sure that your weight is on your left side at the top of the backswing.

ROTATION ERRORS

49

Weight transfer

One of the biggest challenges facing golfers, as they pick up the game for the first time, is to trust that the loft on the club will provide the ball flight they want. It is important that you do not use your body to help the ball into the air. Here, we cover the way in which your weight should move through the swing. The basic rule for the right-hander is this: Your weight should move slightly away from the target in the backswing and toward the target through the downswing. Here's how.

Correct weight transfer

1 With an iron in hand, your weight should be split 50:50 at address. This should be a solid, stable position from where you are able to make an effective weight shift. With a driver or fairway wood in hand, let 60 percent of your weight sit on your right side. This will help you stay behind the ball slightly through impact, finding the optimum ball flight that offers impressive carry.

2 As you take the club back, let your weight edge onto your right side. Importantly, do not sway your upper body to create this weight shift. Just let it move naturally onto your right side.

3 As you reach the top of your backswing, the majority of your weight should be on your right side.

THINK...

**Let your weight move away
from the target on the way
back and toward the target
on the way through.**

Leg drive

Coaches can often be heard saying
that power comes from the
ground. By this, they mean the
way in which your legs use the
ground as a hitting platform. It is
absolutely essential that you use
your legs to drive your weight
toward the target through impact.
Getting stuck on your right side
can cause you to open the clubface
through impact and hit a slice.

Right Drive your weight toward
the target.

4 As you reach impact, your
weight should be moving
toward the target. Notice how the
right foot is off the ground. This is
evidence that your weight is
moving toward the target.

5 To maintain the flow of your swing, your weight should continue
to move toward the target. This will help you release the club
powerfully toward the target, which aids both power and accuracy.

WEIGHT TRANSFER

Transition

Now you have reached the top of your backswing with a full, athletic turn, it is time to turn back toward the ball—this is known as the "transition." The key is not to rush. A smooth transition helps you keep the movements of your arms and upper body in harmony together, avoiding the disasterous effects of a poorly synchronized swing. Master the transition with the following simple steps and drills.

The transition

Common errors

1 This refers to the moment your backswing stops and your downswing starts. Clearly there is a fundamental shift of direction here, so it is important to make this as smooth as possible. As you begin the downswing, your weight begins its drive toward the target.

2 The first part of your body to move toward the target should be your hips. As your hips go, so your upper body and arms will follow. This small "bump" of the hips toward the target is the trigger for the downswing, and everything else will follow in sequence.

STARTING WITH THE RIGHT SHOULDER
Starting down by moving your upper body and, more importantly, your right shoulder is a fatal error that throws the clubhead off-line. This occurs as you become too aggressive, trying to hit the ball instead of swinging through it.

This stop-at-the-top drill is used by a number of top players, including Northern Ireland's young superstar Rory McIlroy. Swing to the top of your backswing and then pause for a fraction of a second. This does two things. First, it ensures that you complete your backswing—players, especially when they have been competing under pressure, often start down too soon, thereby upsetting the coordination of their swing. Second, with a slight pause at the top, you can unleash through the downswing, knowing that everything is correctly in place. Try this drill in practice; it's simple and effective.

THINK...

Keep your transition as smooth as possible and let your hips start the downswing.

Right Stop at the top to make sure the transition is good.

Impact

If your address position, backswing, and transition are all technically sound, your impact position should take care of itself. This is the moment when the clubhead should be moving faster than anywhere else during the swing. If the face is square at impact, your chances of a straight shot are excellent. Here are the keys to a solid impact position. If you take the time to understand them, you'll hit long, straight shots.

Right Your hips should be open and your sternum over the ball.

Far right Make sure that the posture you set at address remains at impact.

The ideal position
Although it is important that you don't try to guide your body into the right position (it should come as part of the natural flow of your swing), you should still know what the correct impact position looks like. Your hips and shoulders should be slightly open, creating room to drive your arms through the ball from inside to outside the ball-to-target line. In the ideal position, the clubface will be pointing directly at the target and your sternum will be directly over the ball. These are the two main differences between the impact and address positions.

Posture
The spine angle you set at address should be exactly the same through impact. This is about consistency of ball striking. If your head does not lift or dip, you will find it far easier to deliver the club cleanly into the back of the ball every time.

DO NOT GUIDE THE CLUB

When you are staring at a tight, tree-lined fairway or a green surrounded by bunkers or water, it can be difficult to commit to your usual, powerful action. This, however, is imperative. By trying to guide the club toward the target, you are far more likely to leave the clubface open through impact, hitting the ball right with a destructive slice. Don't be afraid to hit the ball hard—the golf swing is supposed to be a powerful, dynamic movement.

Weight check

Again, we have already stressed the importance of shifting your weight toward the target through the downswing. At impact, your right heel should be slightly off the ground as the majority of your weight is driven onto your left side. If your weight is set correctly on the balls of your feet at address, you will find it easy to shift your weight during the swing.

Left Your weight should be moving from right to left through impact.

IMPACT

55

Finishing the swing

Your finish position says a lot about the swing that went before it. The best players remain perfectly balanced throughout the swing and are able to hold their finish until the ball lands. However, before we examine the finer details of the finish, it is important to make sure that your action through the ball is also good. This section explains how to master the ideal release and finish. If you can perfect those, your rhythm and timing are guaranteed to improve.

Above Release the club toward the target.

Above A full, balanced finish.

The release

This refers to the way you drive the clubhead toward the target after impact. It is known as the release, as your hands will naturally want to rotate after impact—so let them. A full extension through the ball is the last of the key power moves. Notice how, in the position above, the toe of the club is pointing directly at the sky. This position shows that you have committed fully to the shot and the extension of your arms will naturally force your weight onto your left side. Let your head turn naturally to follow the flight of the ball.

The finish position

If you have made an athletic swing, the momentum of the club will pull you into a full finish position. Get a friend to video or photograph your finish, so you can examine the evidence. An error here is the sign of a more fundamental problem earlier in the motion.

PRACTICE DRILL

If you are having problems holding your finish position, try this drill. Hit a series of practice shots with your feet together. This is one of the oldest drills around but it works perfectly to get your rhythm back, ensuring that you remain balanced all the way through the swing.

THINK...

Release your hands and drive the club toward the target through impact, and swing through to a full, balanced finish.

Weight

Your right heel should be completely off the ground and the majority of your weight should be on the outside of your left foot.

Body position

Your upper body should have rotated through the ball to face the target. Your left knee should be straight because it is around this point that your upper body rotates.

Balance

You should be able to hold this position long after the ball lands. If you are off-balance here, it is evidence of an overly aggressive weight shift.

Right A full, balanced finish position is a sure sign of a technically sound swing.

Checklist

Takeaway, hinge, rotation transition, impact, and the finish are the key moves behind a free flowing swing. Adopt these positions and you'll be more likely to hit your target.

The takeaway

Take the club back directly away from your target line. In this initial move, don't let your wrists hinge or knees bend. A smooth takeaway that is on-line will help you set a good rhythm and swing path.

Wrist hinge

Having taken the club away, hinge your wrists, creating an angle between your forearms and shaft. Halfway through the backswing, the toe of the club should point directly upward and the shaft should run parallel to your ball-to-target line.

Rotation

Turn your upper body 90 degrees, so that your back faces the target and your hips are at 45 degrees. If you hold this position, you should feel the build up of energy that allows you to unwind with speed during the downswing.

Transition

Your move from backswing to downswing should be as smooth as possible. Once you reach the top, let your hips "bump" toward the target. Your lower body will then lead your upper body and arms through the downswing.

Impact

Understand what the perfect impact position should look like. Do not try to guide the club toward the target but drive your body and the clubhead through the ball powerfully.

The finish

Release the club, extending your arms through impact and turning the toe of the club to point skyward half-way through the finish. Your finish position should be balanced with your weight on your left side.

Pitching and chipping

From 100 yards and in, the best players in the world look to get down in two, eight times out of ten. In many ways, it is from this range, often known as "the scoring zone," that great players are able to distinguish themselves. Becoming a good pitcher and chipper requires a deft touch for distance control. This is something that can be honed by spending time practicing at the range and on the course.

However, before you while away the hours developing a deadly natural feel, it is worth establishing some key technical moves. From the full swing of the pitch to the semi-putting motion of the chip-and-run, there are certain basic principles that will help you hit the target.

This chapter will illustrate exactly what to work on and how to do it. If you can master this part of the game, you will always return a decent score, no matter how well your long game is functioning. What follows is a simple guide to being deadly from 100 yards and in.

Equipment advice

Finding a wedge lineup that will allow you to both pitch and chip effectively is worth some careful consideration. Long hitters will benefit more from having three or even four wedges in their bag as these clubs will be used far more often than perhaps a 3-iron. However many wedges you choose, ensure there are even gaps in the lofts between them. For instance, a typical four-wedge lineup might consist of a 48° pitching wedge, a 52° gap wedge, a 56° sand wedge, and a 60° lob wedge. This allows you to cover all the key pitching distances. You will also have a range of different lofts to call upon when faced with delicate chip shots around the green.

All this underlines the importance a comprehensive wedge lineup. If you need more advice before you buy, consult your local PGA professional.

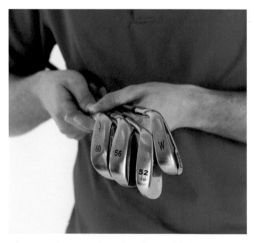

Above Having a number of wedges will help you hit certain key distances.

Right A good pitch is a shorter, more compact, version of the full swing.

Pitching fundamentals

If you have mastered the keys we have already covered for the full swing, there is no reason why you should not become a great pitcher of the ball. There are, however, a few subtle changes both at setup and during the swing. These relate to finding a clean strike and developing a good natural feel for distance control. Above all, you need to find a pitching setup that feels comfortable, is not too rigid, and allows you to chip the ball cleanly away. Here's what you should work on.

Ball position and stance

With a wedge in hand, you have plenty of loft to look down on at address. To ensure you find the ideal, relatively steep angle of attack for a crisp strike, move the ball back a fraction in your stance. Your hands should naturally sit in front of the line of the ball. This technique will help you achieve a clean contact, and it will also ensure that the ball flight is not too high. A controlled flight will help you find the right distance despite any wind that might be blowing. Most players set a slightly narrower stance than usual as the swing does not require the power provided by a wide, stable base. This is about finding a stance that is comfortable for you.

Left The ball should sit a fraction back in your stance.

VARIED PRACTICE

It is always a good idea to practice your pitching with a variety of clubs—not just your wedges. If you can control the flight and distance of every club in the bag, you'll develop a far better, natural feel for the game. It also happens to be a fun way to practice.

THINK...

Move the ball back in your stance a fraction and set your feet closer together than usual.

Leg action

If, indeed, you do choose to set your feet closer together than usual, ensure that your legs remain passive during the swing. An overactive leg action can have disastrous effects on the quality and accuracy of your strikes. Keep a good amount of flex in your knees at address, so that you feel comfortable and athletic and do not let your legs move as you take the club back. A passive leg action is essential for keeping the clubhead on-line.

Right Don't let your lower body sway as you take the club back.

PITCHING FUNDAMENTALS

63

Pitching swing

In many ways, a pitching swing is simply a shorter version of the technique required for a mid-iron shot. However, to pitch well, you need ultimate control both of flight and distance. The tips below will ensure that you remain in charge from start to finish. If you get it right, you'll get up and down from around 100 yards more often than not, and this will have a profound affect on your swing potential.

Backswing

It is important to understand the importance of creating spin. A fast swing and a clean strike will deliver more backspin than a slower motion with a clean contact. You might think that a vast amount of backspin is particularly impressive (it is the sign of a good strike), but too much backspin will cause the ball to balloon into the air. So when you pitch, keep the backswing slightly shorter than usual. Your body turn will be slightly less than usual, as shown, and your subsequent clubhead speed will be reduced.

Right Make a shorter, more compact swing and keep your rhythm smooth.

TRUST THE LOFT AND TAKE A DIVOT

The loft will do all the work required to provide a good flight, so don't feel you need to help the ball into the air by hanging back through impact. Move your weight toward the target through the downswing and don't be afraid to drive through the ball, taking a healthy divot. This will be a natural result of setting the ball back in your stance and finding a steeper angle of attack than usual. A divot is also a sign of a committed approach to the shot.

Through swing

Feel as if you are hitting the ball at 80 percent of your total power—you will automatically find that a slightly curtailed finish position and a smooth action through impact will help control the backspin. As you take some of the power out of your swing, ensure that your weight still transfers toward the target through impact—this is important to achieve the clean contact you are after.

Decelerating toward impact

The biggest mistake when pitching is decelerating the club through the ball. This is sometimes a natural reaction to pressure and it always leads to fat contacts that come up well short of the green. While you are on the course playing in competition, push all the technical thoughts to the back of your mind and concentrate solely on completing the swing. This will help you find a steady build up of pace through impact.

Right Drive your arms and body through impact and into a full finish.

Pitching: Distance control

From inside 100 yards the biggest challenge is controlling your distance. If you get the ball to finish pin high, you'll never be left with a long putt for par or birdie. To master this aspect of the game, you will need a wedge lineup that leaves few distance gaps and a good feel for the power of your own swing. The tips that follow will give you a natural feel for distance and control, helping you get up and down in this crucial area more often.

Three backswing positions

1 On the practice ground, hit 10 or 15 pitch shots by making a half swing with each of your wedges. If possible, measure the distance of the average shot with each wedge. Note these yardages down and these will become your key half swing distances.

2 Now hit 10 or 15 balls, making a three-quarter swing with each of your wedges. Follow the same process, noting down how far the average ball for each wedge went.

3 Now do the same, making a full pitching swing with each shot. You should notice how the extra backspin created by a bigger movement sends the ball higher into the air. Again, note down the average distances. If you have three wedges in your bag, this process will give you nine invaluable yardages.

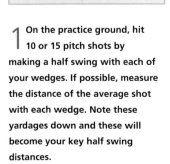

CALCULATING YOUR YARDAGE

Most golf courses will have yardage markers on the fairway that will tell you the distance to the front or middle of the green. Before you head out for a round on a course that you're unfamiliar with, ask the local pro if the yardages are to the front or middle of the greens. When you are on the course, take a minute before you play your pitch to figure out the yardage to the pin. This will help you take on the shot with absolute confidence.

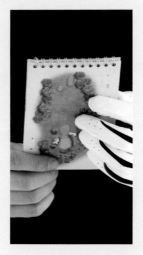

THINK...

Find the pitching yardages you feel comfortable hitting and keep the rhythm of your swing the same, no matter how far back you take the club.

Rhythm control

If you are going to adopt this approach, it is important that the rhythm of your swing remains the same for each pitch shot you play. Be warned that if your rhythm is different for different shots, your distance control will be thrown completely out.

JARGON BUSTING

Pin high When an approach shot finishes level with the distance of the flag.

Right Keep a consistent rhythm and each type of club will offer a different yardage.

Chipping setup

Even the world's finest ball strikers will miss at least two or three greens per round with their approach shots. Being able to rely on a deft chipping touch allows them to keep their score on track and take momentum to the next tee. If you can scramble well, you will be able to turn a bad score into a decent one or a good score into a great one. The importance of developing a sound short game should not be underestimated. Here are the basics to a solid chipping technique.

JARGON BUSTING

Chip-in Holing a chip shot.
Chip-and-run A chip shot that rolls most of the way to the hole.
Lob Where the ball flies most of the way to the hole.
Release After the ball has bounced it "releases" to the hole.
Scrambling The art of chipping and putting.

The setup

1 Take a set-up position that feels comfortable. Allow for a good amount of knee flex and let your hands hang down naturally. Many players prefer to move the ball back slightly in the stance to ensure a clean contact. Ball position here, however, is a matter of personal preference—simply do whatever feels most comfortable.

2 Aim the clubface at the target but set your stance slightly open (aiming fractionally left of the target). This will provide the room for your hands to swing through to the target. Also, be careful not to strangle the grip. Soft hands are essential for a good touch around the greens.

Weight distribution

How your weight is positioned at address, even for these short, delicate shots, can have a big impact on your success. Place a fraction more weight on your left side at address and keep your legs solid through the swing—do not let any weight shift occur. This will help you slip the clubface in tightly behind the back of the ball for a clean contact that delivers plenty of distance, controlling spin.

Above A comfortable, tension-free setup will aid a rhythmical stroke.

Chipping errors

It is a simple equation: Make basic errors at address and you will throw away crucial shots. Here are some of the most commonly seen mistakes. Take a good look at the positions shown below and be careful not to emulate them in your game. These mistakes may seem extreme but these are some of the most commonly seen errors, and they make getting up and down consistently almost impossible.

Weight rooted to left

Mistakes at address often come from taking good advice a little too far. As we have already mentioned, you are supposed to have your weight on your left side at address, but not at the cost of comfortable, balanced posture. Make sure that your weight favors the left instead of being rooted on it. This will upset the fluidity of the strike, and as the club drives steeply in behind the ball you'll risk striking it thin.

Left Setting too much weight on your left side creates a steep angle of attack.

THINK...

Set your weight on your left side but not too far left, let your hands hang ahead of the ball, and point the clubface at your target.

EQUIPMENT ADVICE

There are 14 clubs in your bag and, with the exception of your driver, you should be prepared to use any of them to chip with. Each club has an amount of loft that will help you find a combination of flight and roll, even from just off the green. If you practice chipping with each of your clubs, you will have a vast armory of options at your disposal.

Below Lean back and you risk fat and thin strokes.

Below right Aiming off target is surprisingly easy to do.

Hands behind the ball

The chip shot you are about to play might require a lofted flight, but remember that with a wedge in hand the ball should pop up nicely in the air. Make sure at address that your hands are ahead of the ball. This will help you catch the ball before the turf, guarding against a fat contact.

Bad alignment

Your alignment from close range is something you should be careful to get right. By opening your stance a fraction, you will have the room to swing your arms back and through. As you set your stance, however, ensure that the clubface is pointing directly at the pin.

Chipping swing

A good chipping swing will do two things: set the ball off on the right line and offer you the feel to control the distance of the shot. The next time you practice your short game, spend 30 minutes establishing the key technical points that follow. These simple elements will have a big effect on your scoring potential, and you should notice as you read on how easy they are to adopt. When it comes to chipping—the simpler, the better.

The swing

1 **By setting a solid address position, you will have the best chance of finding a clean contact. Above all, you should be comfortable over the ball— this is a feel shot that requires imagination; it is difficult to have a good touch if your address position is too rigid or tense.**

2 **As you take the club back, allow your wrists to hinge slightly. Some coaches prefer their players to keep their wrists solid, but this can lead to a mechanical stroke that lacks any real feel. A simple rocking of the shoulders will create the momentum you need, and your lower body should remain perfectly still.**

3 **Return to your address position at impact. Notice how passive the leg action remains through this part of the shot. The hands should be slightly ahead of the clubface at this point; this will send the ball off on a low flight with plenty of spin. Maintain a gentle acceleration of the club through impact.**

Above Let your upper body smoothly rotate into the finish position.

Chipping strategy

When planning your chip, pick a spot on the green where you want the ball to land. Visualize the flight and how it will roll once it hits the ground. Now pick the club that will allow you to do that. This simple preparation sets a positive mind-set and will help you plan exactly your best route to the hole.

4 **Let your upper body gradually rotate into the finish position.** Even with a short shot, you should release your upper body to maintain the flow of the stroke. In the ideal position, the sole of the clubhead, your hands, and your upper body will all face the target.

> ### THINK...
> Keep your legs passive and hinge your wrists a fraction on the way back. Ensure that your hands are ahead of the ball at impact, and turn your body to face the target in the finish position.

CHIPPING SWING

Common errors

So you have set the ideal address position—you are comfortable, the ball is in the right position, and your grip pressure is perfectly soft. If you make a simple mistake now, all those important aspects that you have nailed down will be for nothing. Fat and thin contacts will leave you struggling to make bogeys, let alone pars. Take heed of the positions on these pages and be careful not to recreate them—they are sure to leave your scorecard in shambles.

Flicking your wrists

This mistake is made if you try to use a flick of the wrists to get the ball up in the air. Typically, the clubhead will strike the ground a fraction before the ball, causing a thin contact. Allow for a small amount of wrist hinge as you take the club back and then maintain this angle through the ball. Remember to let the club do the work and don't try to help the ball up.

Left Flicking your wrist through impact will kill your distance control.

POOR RHYTHM

In many ways, golf is a game of rhythm. From tee to green, a good tempo will help you find repeatable movements that deliver good results time and again. When you chip, maintain a smooth tempo. Don't rush the shot, jerking at the ball through impact. This will only cause the ball to come out with too much pace. A slow acceleration of the club through impact is ideal.

THINK...

Keep your wrists solid through impact, accelerate the club gently through the ball, and complete your swing.

Decelerating through the ball

The most common problem when chipping is deceleration. This is the sign of a tentative approach and causes a fat contact that leaves the ball well short of its target. When you are on the course, focus on finishing the swing. Picture your finish position and concentrate on swinging through the ball. Don't be afraid to commit to delicate shots; if you play them with soft hands and find a clean strike, you'll have no problem with control.

Left Keep the clubhead moving steadily through impact.

COMMON ERRORS

Practice drills

To sharpen your short game, you need to get down to the practice green and play around with your chipping. To ensure you get the most from this invaluable time, you need some drills that are fun and will instill certain key technical elements. Here is a selection of practice drills to add to your routine—they should improve all the important aspects of your technique while also providing you with a better, instinctive feel for how to play the end shot.

Feel: One-handed chips

The best chippers in the world have an instinctive feel for the shot they are faced with. Like throwing a ball, you take a quick look at the target and then make your swing. Keeping the rhythm of the stroke free and easy will instill this natural feel into your chipping game. To help, hit a series of chips in practice with just one hand. Notice how the momentum you create at the start of the swing smoothly pulls your hand through the stroke. This is the rhythm you need to recreate when chipping with two hands.

THINK...
Your stroke needs a smooth rhythm and your arms and body should work together. Visualize where you want the ball to land and be imaginative by taking on a range of different shots in practice.

Left One-handed chips will improve your feel.

Above Use a towel to help synchronization.

IMAGINATION IS KEY

The best wedge players will see three or four ways of playing each short-game scenario they are presented with. This imagination comes from hours of playing around at the practice putting green. The next time you practice, try to play a variety of different shots from a range of different lies. Without the pressure of building a score on your shoulders, you will develop an instinctive feel for how to manipulate the clubhead to play different shots.

Arms-and-body drill

The more simple your chipping stroke the better, because without any unnecessary movements you will be able to keep the clubhead on-line far easier. To help you with this, place a towel under both armpits and hit a series of shots. The towel should only drop down once your body releases toward the target in the finish position. If it falls down during the backswing or through impact, you will know that your arms and body are not working correctly and that you are probably employing too many unnecessary movements.

Visualization: Landing zones

It is crucial when you chip to map out the shot. Learn how to do this effectively in practice by laying a towel on the green (it can be anywhere from two to ten yards away from you). The aim here is simply to pitch a series of shots onto the towel. At first, this will seem hard to do but as your feel for the shot improves your success rate will improve rapidly.

Right Visualize your landing zone for greater success.

Chip-and-run

It might not seem like the most exciting shot in the book, but if you can develop the right technique for the perfect chip-and-run, it will be invaluable. As long as you do not have sand or thick rough between you and the pin, this is often the safest option. Played with a mid- or even a long iron, the idea here is to bump the ball into the air and let it roll out to the flag. Here's how to play this invaluable shot.

Playing the chip-and-run

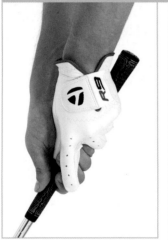

1 Take your normal putting grip. In many respects, you need to think of this shot as a putt, by adopting your putting grip, you will find a better feel for the distance. The ball should sit back slightly in your stance; this will help you find the clean strike you are looking for.

2 Keep your wrists firm as you take the club back. A tiny amount of wrist hinge is fine, but be careful not to use too much as this will add unwanted loft to the shot. You should be able to create a triangle between your shoulders and the clubhead at the top of the backswing. As you take the club back, think "low and slow."

3 Keep your grip pressure soft throughout the stroke. This will give you the free-flowing rhythm you need, ensuring that your feel for the shot is not ruined by a jerky movement through impact.

READ THE GREEN

This chip-and-run is very much like a putt. Around 90 percent of the ball's journey will be on the ground, so it is important to read the green before you play the shot. Remember, as you look at the line, that slopes have a greater effect and the slower the ball rolls, so pay particular attention to any undulations surrounding the hole. Missing these is a frustratingly simple error that can be avoided with an extra moment's consideration as you prepare for the shot.

Club selection

For this particular shot, your aim is to bump the ball into the air and then let it roll out to the hole like a putt. It works really well from just off the green because it takes out the unpredictability of landing the ball in thicker, often roughed-up fringe grass but still gives the reliability of a putt. In this scenario, leave your wedges in the bag and pick a mid- or long iron. The loft you choose depends on how much rough grass you need to carry (the higher the loft, the more long grass you will carry). You can even use your hybrid or fairway woods for this shot—there are no hard and fast rules. Just pick the club that offers the best combination of flight and roll.

Right Think about just how much rough you need to carry.

Checklist

Your ability to pitch and chip will determine your scoring potential. Now that you know what the right technique consists of, use this checklist to make sure old habits don't creep in.

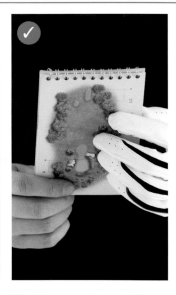

Pitching setup

Move the ball back in your stance fractionally to ensure you create the ideal descending angle of attack. Your address position should be comfortable and maintain the same posture as with any full shot. As always, don't allow tension to creep in at address; this will only disrupt the fluidity of the stroke.

Pitching swing

Never swing with full force when you pitch. This will create excess backspin at impact, which pops the ball up too high into the air making distance very difficult to judge, especially if you have any wind to contend with. Keep your legs more passive than usual and release your upper body to face the target in the finish.

Pitching practice drills

Head to the range and figure out how far you hit each wedge in your bag; these will become your key lay-up yardages, so take the time to note them down. Make sure that your rhythm remains the same, no matter which club you choose and how far the shot is.

Chipping setup

Find a comfortable set-up position and let your hands hang down naturally. Aim your feet slightly left of the target with your clubface directly toward where you want the ball to land. Place slightly more weight on your left side at address to ensure a clean contact.

Chipping swing

Allow for a small amount of wrist hinge as you take the club back. Keep your body over the ball through the stroke and allow your upper body to rotate toward the target in the finish position. Again, a passive leg action will help you keep the clubhead on line through the shot.

Chipping practice drills

Hit a series of shots one-handed to help the rhythm of your stroke and improve your natural feel. Place a towel on the green to mark your landing zone to improve your visualization of the shot. To help you groove a simple motion, place a towel under both armpits. This keeps your arms and body working as one.

Putting

Putting is often thought of as the game within a game. Your success with a putter in hand is the catalyst that turns what you do with the rest of your clubs into cold, hard numbers. The tips and drills that follow have been designed to make this part of your game as simple and effective as possible. So where better to start than with the basics of grip and ball position?

The grip

1 There are many ways to grip the putter. As long as you feel comfortable at address and confident that you can swing back and through on a repeatable line, you can choose any grip you like. However, the overlapping version shown here is perhaps the most popular option.

2 Start by placing your left hand on the club, so your thumb points straight at the putter head. Place your right hand below the left, but make sure the palms of your hands face each other. Place your left index finger on top of the fingers of your right hand and keep both your thumbs on top of the center of the grip.

Ball position

Where the ball sits relative to your feet can make as big a difference on the green as with a driver in hand. Ideally, the ball should sit just forward of center, so the putter strikes the ball slightly on the upswing. This has the effect of creating a small amount of topspin at impact, which, in turn, causes a stronger rolling putt that will not be bumped off-line by any imperfections on the green. To find out where the ideal ball position is, take your normal address position, then drop a ball from your left eye—where it hits the ground is where the ball should sit in relation to your stance.

Right Set the ball slightly forward in your stance for a better roll.

The stroke

The key to success is simplicity. A stroke that moves back and through on a consistent line or slight arc will set the ball rolling on your intended line, although some players prefer a more natural curved stroke that mirrors the opening and closing of a door. At the moment of impact, the clubface should be absolutely square to your target; if not, the only time you will hole putts is when you misread the green. A simple technique will keep the putter on line and offer a high level of feel.

The basic stroke

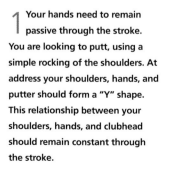

1 Your hands need to remain passive through the stroke. You are looking to putt, using a simple rocking of the shoulders. At address your shoulders, hands, and putter should form a "Y" shape. This relationship between your shoulders, hands, and clubhead should remain constant through the stroke.

2 Create the momentum in your stroke by rocking your shoulders. Like when you chip, allow for a very small amount of hinge in your wrists— this will maintain the flow of the stroke without creating any unwanted loft.

3 If the ball is forward slightly in your stance at address, you will strike it slightly on the upswing, creating topspin. Notice here how the player's head has remained perfectly still. Do not lift your head to see where the ball has gone until after impact. If you do, you'll come out of the stroke too early and miss it to the right.

WEAR A GLOVE?

If you are a regular follower of professional golf, you will notice that the majority of players take their glove off to putt. This can give you a better feel for the weight of the club in your hands. However, this is simply a matter of personal preference. The greatest player of all time, Jack Nicklaus, always putted with his glove still on!

THINK...

Keep your head still and maintain the "Y" shape between your shoulders and the club throughout the stroke. Gently accelerate through the ball and finish the stroke.

Below Once you've picked your line, concentrate on making a solid, simple stroke.

4 **Let the putter head drive through toward the target, as** this will help you make a committed, free-flowing stroke. Notice how the player's posture is the same in the finish position as at address. By staying down over the ball, you will find a better quality and accuracy of strike.

THE STROKE

Long putting

A good natural feel for the pace of the greens will help you roll the ball up to the hole consistently from long distances. This is crucial to good scoring because no matter how good your long game, you will always face a few long putts in every round you play. The closer to the hole you leave it, the less stressful your round will be. To do this successfully, you need two things: a solid technique and a deft touch. These tips will help you in both areas.

The long putt

1 **Your address position is much the same as when putting** from short range. The only slight alteration you may want to make is to widen your stance a fraction. A solid base is crucial on the greens, and, by widening your stance, you will guard against any unwanted leg action, which can easily creep in on longer putts.

2 **The rhythm of your stroke should remain the same from** the first to the 18th green. To control the distance, simply take the club back slightly farther. You may also need to hinge your wrists a little more than usual. This is fine; just make sure you don't hinge them too much.

3 **Through impact, your body needs to be perfectly still.** When faced with a longer putt, players will often try to use their bodies to help the ball on its way. Try to avoid doing this, as excess body movement will only bump the stroke off-line.

KEEP YOUR EYES SHUT

Make a series of practice strokes with your eyes shut. Start by taking a good look at the putt you are faced with. Now close your eyes and make a series of practice swings. Feel how far your hands should swing to achieve the distance you want. This helps develop an instinctive feel, which is essential when playing any delicate shots around the green.

THINK...

Widen your stance a fraction and make a slightly longer stroke than usual. Before you play, try to develop a natural feel for the putt.

Right Look at the hole and make a series of practice swings to get a feel for pace.

Look at the hole

Add this to your preshot routine and you will develop a good feel for the pace of the greens. Stand behind the ball, look at the hole and then your ball, and make a series of practice strokes, trying to find the right length of backswing for the putt. Your brain will process the relationship between the distance to the hole and the strength of the stroke required. Without thinking specifically about it, you will develop a far more natural feel for the pace of the putt. Try it for yourself, and you'll see how well it works.

LONG PUTTING

Short putting

At times, golf can seem to be the cruellest of sports. What feels and looks like the easiest task imaginable, holing out from inside 3 feet, can often seem almost impossible. This is the area where you need to control your mind and trust the fundamentals you have already put into play. Confidence is key from short range, as a tentative stroke will end in disaster. Here's how to approach those horrible 3-footers.

How hard?

There are different theories relating to how hard you should hit your short putts. First, you need to understand that the faster the ball is rolling when it reaches the hole, the more likely it is to lip out. However, if you are unsure how the putt will break, aim at the center of the cup and hit the ball firmly. If you are confident with the break, look to roll the ball in at a gentle pace—it should drop, no matter what part of the hole it hits.

The short putt

1 Having taken a moment to read the putt, you will know where you want to start the ball rolling. At address, pick a spot on this line and simply concentrate on sending the ball over this point.

2 If you are tentative on the greens, your short-range putting will suffer. That's why it is imperative that you complete your stroke. Drive the putter through to the target without lifting your upper body. If you can do this, your short-range putting stats will be the key to good scoring.

PRACTICE DRILL

This excellent round-the-clock drill, with a number of balls set in a circle around a hole, as shown, is used by many of the world's best players. The idea here is to hole each ball consecutively—do not finish until you have completed the challenge. As the angle for each putt changes, the task is slightly different every time. This drill also re-creates the kind of pressure you will feel on the course. Coming to terms with pressure is crucial, especially when it comes to putting from close range.

THINK...

Pick a spot on your line and concentrate on rolling the ball over this point. Finish the stroke and keep your body down.

Left Pick a spot on your line and roll the ball towards the target.

Preshot routine

As we have already touched upon, the game on the greens is as much a mental challenge as a physical one. A preshot routine will help you to slip into autopilot whenever the pressure builds. The following routine will help you find an instinctive feel and a good line. If you can use this routine for every putt you hit, the whole process will become second nature and you'll hit good putts time and again under pressure.

Establishing a routine

1 Start with a thorough read of the putt. Take your first look as you arrive on the green, thinking about all the general slopes on the putting surface. Look at the putt from at least two angles: usually from behind the hole and behind the ball. Pay particular attention to the slopes around the hole—as the ball runs out of speed, they will have a greater effect.

2 The time has come to make a few practice swings. You can either do this alongside the ball or behind it looking at the hole. It is important that you do two things: rehearse a smooth rhythm, which will help you control the pace of the putt; and use this as an opportunity to develop a feel for the length of the stroke.

3 Now take your address position. Do not rush as this can lead to avoidable mistakes. Make sure that your body is set square to where you want the ball to start rolling. Take one last look at the hole and then pull the trigger. Once you are in the right position, do not wait, as unwanted tension will soon start to creep in.

The key here is repetition. You can really employ any routine you like as long as it is the same every time. The routine shown will help you find a good line and set your stance square, but if it does not work for you, don't worry. Play with the routine until you find something you are confident with. A strong mind-set lies at the heart of any preshot routine.

Read the putt, make a few practice swings, set your body square to your target, and then pull the trigger.

Practice your routine

It might sound like a somewhat boring exercise, but any time you are on the practice putting green, use a preshot routine for each shot you hit. The more you run through your routine, the more ingrained it will become. As the pressure mounts on the course, this simple set of moves will help you feel both comfortable and confident. Every top player has a preshot routine—you should too!

Right Your preshot routine will be invaluable whenever you play in competition.

Reading putts

On the face of it, reading putts seems incredibly easy. Look at the green and pick the slopes—how hard can it be? The answer will depend on the green. The hardest greens to read are those with subtle slopes. Seeing how these will shape the run of the putt is the art of good green reading. The tips that follow will show you how to examine the green to pick up on the obvious and not-so-obvious slopes, while also developing an exact feel for how your specific putt will break.

Above As you walk onto the green, look at the breaks on the putting surface as a whole.

Above Look at your putt from different spots on the green to get a better feel for the break.

Read as you approach

As you approach the green, look at the putting surface as a whole. Players often get drawn into looking at the line of their putt, missing the bigger clues available. For example, if there is water around the green, it makes sense that any putt will break slightly toward the water.

Take a walk

Players often find that walking around the green gives them a feel for where the slopes are. By treading the territory, you might be able to pick up on some key slopes that you would not otherwise have picked up on.

As we have already mentioned, visualization is a great way to prepare for any shot. One way to employ this as you read the green is to imagine pouring a bucket of water onto the green from your ball. Picture the water trickling away. By visualizing the water, you will see all the key slopes surrounding your ball.

Below If you are going to miss, make sure you miss on the high side of the hole.

Above If the wind is blowing hard, take a wider stance at address.

Is there a strong wind?

Strong winds should be taken into account when you read a putt. They will almost certainly have an impact, especially if the green itself is exposed.

Give it enough room to break

A common mistake that amateur golfers make is never giving a putt enough room to break. If you think you will miss a putt, try to miss it on the high side of the hole, as this means the ball is always turning toward the hole and has a chance of dropping instead of slipping away from the cup.

Reading grain

Some courses can throw an extra element at you—grain. This is when the grass grows during the day but leans toward the sun; the grain can cause the putt to move. The basic rule here is that if the grass looks shiny between you and the hole, you are putting down grain and it will be very quick. If the grass is darker, you will be putting into the grain, so you'll need to hit the ball a little harder. Remember that grain only really comes into consideration when playing in hot, wet climates.

READING PUTTS

93

Putting drills

Practicing your putting does not need to involve a series of boring processes. All the drills on these pages have been designed to improve the technical aspects of your putting, while offering an element of competition or enjoyment to keep you interested throughout. Add these to your regular routine and your scores will reflect this sound training. There are plenty of enjoyable games you can play that will improve your success rate.

Through-the-gate drill

This simple and effective drill is designed to ensure the putter works back and through on a straight path. Place two shafts on the ground, fractionally wider than the width of your putter. Now hit a series of putts. With the shafts acting as a guide, your stroke will quickly become more consistent. If you prefer to make an arced stroke, simply place two tee pegs in the ground fractionally wider than the head of your putter. At the moment of impact, the putter should swing through this "gate" without making contact.

Left Create a narrow channel to develop a solid straight back and through stroke.

Tee-peg drill

This is an easy way to improve your focus on the greens. Instead of putting to a hole, place a tee peg in the ground and putt to that. At first, you will find it hard to hit, but your strike rate will rapidly improve. Once you've hit 10 or 15 putts, return to putting at a hole. Compared with the tee, it will seem like the size of a bucket and you will feel as if you can't possibly miss! This is a great drill to use before you play in a competitive round.

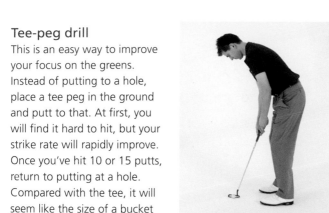

Left Narrow your focus by putting to a tee.

Below Use the box drill to hone you pace.

Box drill

An element of competition is always good to add to your putting routine because the more comfortable you feel when the heat is on the better. For this drill, create a three-sided box, using three shafts around a hole, as shown. Now putt toward the hole from around 25 yards. If the ball finishes short of the hole, you get minus two points. If it finishes level or beyond the hole, without striking the shaft at the back, you get five points. If you hit the shaft at the back, you get minus two points, and if you miss the box completely, it's minus five. Test yourself by recording your scores at various stages of the season. This drill creates pressure and focuses your mind on finding the perfect speed—essential for putting from long distances.

Checklist

Putting is often described as a game within a game. Now that you've established the key aspects to a good technique, use this handy checklist to make sure that bad habits do not creep in.

Grip and posture

Take a grip that is comfortable and allows your hands to sit on the club without too much tension. Set your posture so that your eyes are over the ball at address and your hands hang down naturally.

The stroke

There are two common theories to choose from when it comes to the stroke. You can either opt for a straight back-and-through motion, keeping the clubhead on-line with the target throughout or, alternatively, the stroke can have a slight arc as your arms rotate around your body. Allow for a very small amount of wrist hinge as you take the club back, and keep your body as still as possible throughout the stroke.

Long putting

Control the distance by making a longer stroke and maintaining a smooth rhythm with a steady acceleration through impact. Make a series of practice strokes from behind the ball while looking at the hole; this will give you a more instinctive feel for the shot you are about to play.

Short putting

Narrow your focus by looking at an exact spot either on the grass in front of you or in the back of the hole to roll the ball over. Be positive—this is where any mental frailties will appear, so concentrate on completing your stroke with a positive acceleration of the putter head toward the hole.

Routine

To help you cope with the nervous tension, use a simple pre-shot routine. A routine that helps you set a solid address position is always preferable but not essential. Repeat the routine for every putt you face and you will be able to switch into autopilot when the pressure mounts.

Reading greens

Take a look at the green as a whole and identify where all the major slopes are. Take a look at your putt from a couple of different angles, and pay close attention to slopes around the hole as these will affect your putt the most.

Troubleshooting

Golf courses are filled with danger. Sand, trees, water, and thick rough are the green keepers' way of protecting their courses from a barrage of slow scores. The demands of these different situations vary greatly, from a high-flying, soft-landing greenside bunker shot to an approach shot from a sidehill lie. This chapter will show you how to cope with all those scenarios that threaten a good score.

Greenside bunker setup

Right From a greenside bunker, aim to strike the sand an inch before the ball.

1 Aim the clubface directly at the target but set your feet, hips, and shoulders slightly open to your ball-to-target line. Shuffle your feet in the sand to find a more secure stance. The ball should sit forward in your stance just inside your left heel.

2 When playing from sand, you aren't actually trying to strike the ball cleanly. By moving the ball forward, you ensure that you will catch the sand an inch or so before the ball. Set more of your weight on your right side than usual; if you remain on your back foot slightly through impact, you will add loft to the shot.

Taking your grip

If you find your ball in a greenside bunker, you will need to pop it up in the air, so it clears the lip of the bunker and lands softly on the green. For this, you should open the face of your sand wedge a fraction. Turn the top of the grip to the right and the face will open (the leading edge will also point fractionally right) and then take your shot. The extra loft that you have created here will help you commit to the shot by hitting it hard without losing control of it.

Greenside bunker swing

Having set the correct address position, you are well placed to slide the face of your wedge underneath the ball for a high-flying, soft-landing escape. Now your attention should switch to developing the ideal technique for the swing itself. This will take time to master during practice, but to play 18 holes without visiting a single bunker is extremely rare. The tips on this pages are the key to playing the splash shot well.

The swing

1 **Having opened your body to the ball-to-target line, take the club back on the line of your body and not the line of the target—this helps you cut across the ball through impact, adding crucial extra loft. Start your swing by hinging your wrists, as shown. This is what creates the loft during the swing itself.**

2 **Swing aggressively through impact and strike the sand an inch or two before the ball. Notice here how the player's posture remains the same as at address. Unlike a normal full shot, your weight should be set more on your back foot through impact—this helps you add loft to the shot.**

3 **As you accelerate the clubhead through impact, you should find that your body drives through to the full finish position naturally. Your chest should be facing the target, with your balance perfectly intact. If you can complete your swing every time, you will guard against a disastrous deceleration.**

SPLASH MARK

The splash your club makes in the sand can tell you a lot about the shot you've just played. Ideally, the splash should be shallow and around 10 cm (4 inches) long. If you can re-create this splash every time, consistency will be the key to your success in the sand.

THINK...

Hinge your wrists as you take the club back, maintain your posture through impact, and swing through to a full, balanced finish position.

Below Be aggressive from sand by driving the club powerfully through impact.

Greenside bunker drills

Repetition is the key to success from greenside bunkers. If you can find a swing that repeats time and again, striking the sand at the perfect point, you will get up and down with ease. These drills are designed to help you develop the perfect motion that will deliver the ball with a cushion of sand. The circle-in-the-sand drill is a good place to start when it comes to bunkers; you'll soon realize that you don't need to strike the ball to find consistent success.

Circle-in-the-sand drill

1 Draw a circle around your ball as shown. Now take your usual address position with the clubface open to your stance.

2 Don't worry about the specific technique but simply try to drive your club through the circle, taking all the sand that is within it.

Throw the sand at the hole

As we have already mentioned, the idea is to hit the sand before the ball. This means that you can be aggressive from sand without hitting the ball too far. To illustrate this point, find a bunker that is fairly close to the flag, around 15 yards (14 metres) away, and hit a number of shots. Don't worry about where the ball finishes but aim solely to hit the sand as far as the hole. You'll find that you can be as aggressive as you like with the swing without losing control of the shot.

Line-in-the-sand drill

1 Take the bunker rake and use the butt end to draw a line in the sand, horizontal to your ball-to-target line. Now place five balls along this line.

2 Work your way up the line and hit each of the five balls quickly. Once you have finished, take a look at the line in the sand. Each splash should start an inch before the line and finish an inch after it. If you can develop this crucial impact characteristic, bunkers will pose no real threat to your score.

Greenside bunker errors

The mistakes that are highlighted here are simple ones that will cost you shots. As ever, if you are careful when setting the key fundamentals, avoiding the errors featured below, there is no reason why you should not escape sand with success every single time you play. If you ever find yourself struggling from sand, return to these pages and you should discover the error that is costing you shots and advice on how to avoid it.

Closed clubface at impact

This is one of the simplest but most common errors when playing from sand. The mistake comes from taking your grip and then attempting to open the face. All that you'll do is change your hand position at address. Through impact, the clubface will return to being closed and you will not generate the loft required to escape a steep greenside bunker lip.

> **THINK...**
> Open the clubface at address, swing along the line of your body, and accelerate the clubhead through impact for a committed stroke.

Right Make sure that the clubface is pointing at the target through impact.

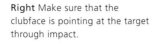

Not hitting along your body line

Having set your body open to the target at address, it is crucial that you swing along the line of your body and not the target line. As the club moves through impact, it should travel from outside to inside the ball-to-target line—this helps you create loft. If you swing along the line of your body, bad strikes and low flights could leave you playing your next shot from the same bunker.

Left Swing the clubhead along the line of your body.

Below Keep the clubhead driving powerfully through the sand at impact.

USE THE TECHNOLOGY

Your sand wedge is designed to help you escape from bunkers. The wide sole creates an angle between the leading edge of the blade and back edge of the sole, which is called "bounce." In fact, the back edge of the sole should strike the sand first. It is this part of the club that allows it to bounce through the sand and not dig in, maintaining crucial momentum through impact. Use the bounce to your advantage by always ensuring the back of the sole strikes the sand first.

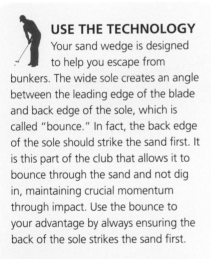

Decelerating toward impact

With any greenside shot, decelerating through impact is often a natural response to nervous tension, but this will cause you to hit the shot fat, leaving the ball in the sand. At address, concentrate on swinging through to a full finish; this will help you find the gentle acceleration you need.

Fairway bunkers

A few simple setup alterations, some sensible club selection, and good tactics will help you escape the potential danger posed by a fairway bunker. At first glance, that 150-yard (137-metre) plus bunker shot may seem impossible, but there is no reason why you should not still be able to find a clean, crisp contact. The tips that follow are designed to ensure you catch the ball before the sand, and return to safety without fairway bunkers costing you shots.

Fairway bunker setup

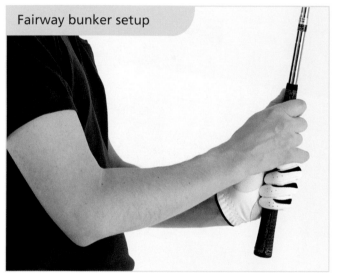

1 The aim of this shot is to catch the ball cleanly, taking as little sand as possible. A thin contact here is actually ideal, so grip the club tighter than usual. This will tense up the muscles in your forearms, creating a more compact swing that catches the ball fractionally thin. First, do not shuffle your feet in the sand—this will only lower your center of gravity, making it harder to find a thin strike. Grip down the club a fraction, so that the thumb of your right hand sits on the bottom of the grip. Set the same posture as you would for any full shot.

2 Once you have settled on your tactics, it is time to commit to the shot. Anything less than 100 percent conviction will cause you to come up way short of your target. As you practice, consider the key swing tips that follow and you should be able to find the clean contact required.

Left Keep your height through impact for a good strike.

The swing

THINK...

Grip down the shaft a fraction, squeeze the grip, and set your usual posture. Rotate your upper body as you take the club back, maintaining the posture you set at address, and hit down and through the ball. Drive through to a full finish position.

1 The swing is a "quiet" swing; you are striking the ball with an energetic upper body but a slightly more stable lower body. You want to make as little contact with the sand as possible through impact. Your posture should be the same here as at impact.

2 As always, it is important to drive through to a full finish position. Your weight should be on your left side and you should be balanced enough to hold this stance until the ball lands.

FAIRWAY BUNKERS

Playing from a divot

There is nothing more frustrating than splitting the fairway with a perfectly struck drive only to find your ball lying in a divot. This poses a significant threat to a good strike, so you will need to be careful. The good news is that, with a few simple adjustments, you can still escape with a par. The address position below should be used whenever you find your ball sitting down, whether it is on the fairway or in the rough.

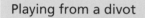

Playing from a divot

1 Your posture and stance width should be the same as usual, but move the ball back in your stance (just inside your right heel) and move a fraction more of your weight onto your left side. It is important to let your hands hang down naturally, so they are ahead of the ball at address.

2 As you take the club back, hinge your wrists early. This creates a steep angle of attack, allowing you to strike the ball before the turf. In this position, keep your weight centered. Again, this will help you to strike down without your body getting too far ahead of the ball at impact.

3 Make no mistake: This is an aggressive shot. You should feel as if you are punching the ball out of its divot. If you hit down into the back of the ball correctly, you will create a healthy divot. Drive your weight onto your left side through the downswing and keep your body over the ball at impact.

PREDICT THE FLIGHT

Having set the ball back in your stance at address and by hitting down on the ball, you will deloft the club you are using. This means that a 7-iron shot will adopt the kind of flight you would expect to see from a 6- or even 5-iron. So as you select your club, allow for a lower flight with more roll once it hits the ground.

4 Your finish position will naturally be shorter than usual. This is fine, but your body should still have rotated to face the target and your weight should be firmly on your right side. You should be perfectly balanced in this position.

Above Why not master this shot on the practice ground?

THINK...

Move the ball back in your stance, hinge your wrists early, and hit down on the ball.

PLAYING FROM A DIVOT

Thick rough

Every course you play will have areas of thick rough. If you find yourself in here, you will have to make a difficult decision about how aggressive you should be. To hit the green from thick rough requires skill and a powerful, committed approach to the shot. A weak swing is sure to cost you shots. So whether you decide to go for it or lay up, here's how to find a powerful shot from deep rough.

Playing from the rough

1 First, assess the lie. If the lie is terrible, move the ball back in your stance (just inside your left heel) and place the majority of your weight on your left side. If the lie is OK, the ball should sit toward the center of your stance and your weight should be more evenly split.

2 Hinge your wrists early in the swing to create a steep angle of attack as you would when playing from a divot (see page 108). Allow yourself room to roll the ball toward your target as you will generate no backspin from thick grass.

3 As when playing from a divot, this needs to be a muscular shot. If the ball is sitting down in particularly dense grass you may need all your strength to get it out. This is one of the only occasions in the game when thoughts of a smooth rhythm are not necessarily helpful. Be aggressive.

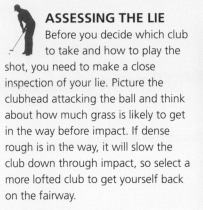

ASSESSING THE LIE

Before you decide which club to take and how to play the shot, you need to make a close inspection of your lie. Picture the clubhead attacking the ball and think about how much grass is likely to get in the way before impact. If dense rough is in the way, it will slow the club down through impact, so select a more lofted club to get yourself back on the fairway.

Right Be careful from thick rough—don't be too ambitious.

Hitting from slopes

Rarely will you find your ball sitting on a perfectly flat lie. Subtle undulations add an extra layer of difficulty as they will naturally change the way the club works through impact. The important thing to remember is not to fight these slopes. Allow for the alteration, changing your club selection and approach to the shot accordingly. As long as you know what to expect, playing from slopes is straightforward.

The swing for an uphill lie

1 An uphill lie automatically adds loft to your club, so take an extra club and be prepared for a high-flying approach. At address, set your shoulders parallel to the slope. Keep your weight centered and allow for a decent amount of knee flex, so that you are in a comfortable position before you take the club away.

2 Make a normal backswing, maintaining a good rhythm and balance. The slope will tend to push your weight onto your right side; be careful of this and try to stay centered over the ball.

3 Drive through impact as you would do from a flat lie. Make sure your weight is moving onto your left side and find a balanced finish position.

Uphill lies

When your ball sits on an upslope, the terrain will severely alter your address position. You need to make some key adjustments to your technique to ensure the ball doesn't balloon too high into the air. Here's how to do it.

Downhill lies

A downslope naturally pushes your weight onto your left side. Finding a clean crisp strike in this position requires a series of subtle changes.

THINK...

Set your shoulders parallel to the slope and let the flex in your knees take up the gradient. Remember that from an uphill lie the trajectory will be far higher, and the reverse applies when playing from a downhill lie.

The swing for a downhill lie

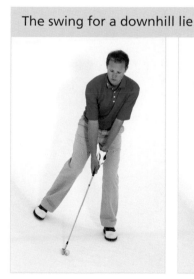

1 **Set your shoulders square to the slope, so the shaft of the** club runs at 90 degrees to the slope. Allow your right shoulder to flex a fraction more than usual to take the gradient of the slope.

2 **Pick up the club steeply and try to keep your weight** evenly spread throughout the swing and don't fight the slope. As when playing from a divot, a steeper angle of attack will cause the ball to come out on a far lower trajectory than usual.

3 **What ever you do, don't lean back to try and lift the ball** into the air. Stay down over the ball through impact and drive your weight onto your left side as you would normally do.

LESSON 6

Sidehill lies

When you play from an uphill or downhill lie the trajectory changes, but from a sidehill lie it is the shape of the shot that is different. With the ball above your feet, you will be forced to make a more rounded swing than usual. This creates right-to-left sidespin at impact, which causes the ball to shape to the left through the air. When the ball is below your feet, the swing will naturally become more "up and down." This has the opposite effect: left-to-right spin, which causes the ball to shape to the right through the air. Again, it is best not to fight the slope but allow it to move the ball naturally through the air.

Ball below feet

This is the sloping lie that players find harder to combat than any other. The key swing and setup changes that follow will help you stay down over the ball and commit to an accurate shot.

Ball above feet

With the ball above your feet, a more rounded swing is inevitable. If you don't know how to cope with the resulting ball flight, a wayward approach is on the cards. Follow these key changes to make an accurate contact.

The swing for a sidehill lie

1 **This is a tough shot, so be careful with your address position. Grip up the shaft slightly, increasing the length of the club. Bend more at your hips than usual to lower your upper body over the ball. This will help you find a clean contact.**

2 **Aim a fraction left of your target to allow for the left to right at impact. Do not let your upper body lift or dip during the backswing—this would have disastrous results on the strike.**

3 **Stay down over the ball through impact and complete the swing as usual. It is incredibly difficult to maintain your balance in the finish, so do not worry if you have to take a step to steady yourself.**

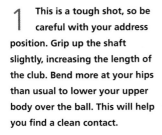

THINK...

Alter your posture to ensure that your upper body is perfectly over the ball throughout the swing. Don't fight the slope but allow for the inevitable shot shape.

Left Aim right when the ball is above your feet.

Far left Aim left when the ball is below your feet.

The swing for ball above feet

1 **Grip down the shaft an inch more than usual and** take a more upright posture at address. Your weight will automatically fall onto your heels. Don't worry about this; just make sure that your address position is athletic enough to make a full turn on the backswing.

2 **Now make a normal swing. It will be more rounded than** usual, so aim slightly right to allow for the right-to-left shape through the air.

3 **Stay down through the ball, transfer your weight to the** left through impact, and swing through to a full finish position. Do not be tentative through the shot but make a powerful release through impact. If you attempt to guide the ball toward the target, you will only hit it left.

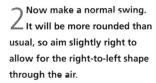

Checklist

A round of golf will have you facing a rage of unexpected situations, including bunkers, divots, rough, and slopes. Use the checklist below for a quick reminder of what to do.

Bunker swing

Take the club back by hinging your wrists and aim to strike the sand an inch or two before the ball. Accelerate the club through to a full finish position in which your chest should face the target.

Fairway bunker swing

Maintain the posture you set at address through to impact. Hit down into the back of the ball and drive through to a normal finish position. Try to take as little sand as possible through impact.

Playing from a divot

Set the ball back in your stance and take the club back by hinging your wrists. With a fraction more weight on your left side at address you should create a steeper angle of attack into the ball for a solid strike.

Thick rough
Be aggressive when playing from thick rough and do not be too ambitious with your club selection. Picture the club moving through impact to help you assess the lie and how to play the shot.

Hitting from slopes
Set your shoulders square to the slope and let your knees take up the gradient in the slope. From an uphill lie, allow for a higher flight; and from a downhill lie, the ball will come out on a lower trajectory with more roll.

Sidehill lies
When the ball is below your feet, allow for a left-to-right shot shape; when the ball is above your feet it will fly right to left through the air. Find a comfortable address position and then make a full and committed swing.

Advanced long game

No two golf courses are the same and on any given day the challenges you face are likely to be slightly different. Being versatile enough to adjust your game to meet these unique challenges should be your next goal. In this lesson, we will examine how to shape shots and hit the ball high and low as well as illustrating some handy short-game alternatives.

So no matter if the pin is tucked away behind a bunker or water or if you are playing in a 30-mph wind, you will have a way of keeping your score intact. By learning these advanced skills, you will also better understand how to manipulate the club throughout the swing. Simply, the tips that follow will boost your scoring potential.

Hitting a fade

"Fade" is the term used to describe a shot that moves gently from left to right through the air. Many top players rely on this shape under pressure, as this is a safe, reliable option. To hit a fade, you need to manipulate the clubface angle and swing path.

Opposite Swing along the line of your body but keep the club pointing at the target.

The fade

1 Address the ball, aiming the clubface at the target but with your feet, hips, and shoulders open to your ball-to-target line. Take time to set this position correctly because getting this right is the key to finding a gentle left-to-right shape.

2 Now start your swing. It's important to take the club back on the line of your body and not directly on a line away from your target as usual. By swinging along the line of your body, the clubface will naturally be open at impact, creating the sidespin you want.

Hitting a draw

A powerful shot, a "draw" refers to when the ball starts right and moves gently back toward its target. The right-to-left spin created at impact produces this impressive flight. A draw will help you work your ball around obstacles or into tight pins. To master this shot, you need to make some simple adjustments to your address position and commit to the strike. Trust the technique described on these pages and you'll master the petite but immensely powerful draw.

The draw

1 Carefully aim the clubface directly at the target. Now aim your feet, hips, and shoulders to the right of the target. As you look down at address you should feel as if your body and clubface are pointing in slightly different directions.

2 Now make a normal swing. As when hitting a fade, be careful to ensure you swing the club along the line of your body and not directly away from the target on the target line as you would normally do.

3 Unlike hitting a fade (when you should keep the clubface pointing at the target for a fraction longer than usual), a draw requires a full effective release. Feel as if the back of your glove is pointing at the ground halfway into the follow-through. This is a powerful position that helps add extra yards to the shot.

THINK...

Aim the clubface at the target and set your feet, hips, and shoulders closed to your ball-to-target line. Swing the club along the line of your body and make a powerful release through impact.

What's the difference?

So, you may ask, what is the difference between a fade and a slice and a draw and a hook. Essentially, these shots shape the same way through the air, but a slice and a hook are more aggressive, destructive versions when the ball shapes too much.

Prepare for the shot

A draw will travel on a lower flight and go farther than a normal shot. Players opt for this when they are looking to attack a flag on the left side of the green or find a few extra yards off the tee.

HITTING A DRAW

121

Trajectory control

Only occasionally will you play golf in completely calm conditions. Wind is a common factor that should come into your consideration before you play the vast majority of your shots. When the wind is strong, you may find that manipulating the flight is the only way to control the shot. The ability to play a low punch will prove invaluable, the more golf you play. It is often the safest option as it takes the wind out of play.

The low punch shot

1 Move the ball back in your stance, so it sits just inside your right heel at address. It is important that your hands still hang down naturally. This creates an angle between the shaft and the ground. Place 60 percent of your weight on your left side at address.

2 Make a slightly shorter swing than usual and keep 60 percent of your weight on your left side. Ensure that you still rotate your upper body— failure to do so could lead to an unsynchronized downswing and wayward shot.

3 Hit down into the back of the ball. By setting your weight on your left side and the ball back at address, you will find a steeper angle of attack than usual through impact, delofting the club for a lower flight than usual.

ADDING LOFT

This is a tougher relative of the punch that should only be taken on if you are confident you can pull it off. To add loft, move the ball forward in your stance a fraction at address and set more weight on your right side. Make a normal swing but be aggressive through impact to add extra backspin to the shot. Don't hold back—good clubhead speed is the key to a high flight. Swing through to a full finish and you should produce a higher flight. Make sure that you release the club as usual through impact—failure to do so will cause a destructive slice. This shot can be helpful when playing downwind as a high drive will provide impressive distance.

THINK...

Move the ball back in your stance, set your weight on your left side, and make a shorter, softer swing than usual.

Below Move your hands down the grip a fraction for a lower flight.

4 Your follow-through should be shorter than usual. Remember that too much backspin will cause the ball to balloon, so swing at 80 percent to find a flatter, more penetrating flight.

TRAJECTORY CONTROL

123

Flop shot

Your approach shot to the green has drifted away from your target and come to rest behind a bunker. The flag is only a few yards away on the green the other side. So, what do you do? The answer is to play a flop shot. This is a high-flighted chip that carries the sand, rough, or any other obstacles between you and the green and stops quickly next to the flag. Sometimes a flop shot is your only option. Here's how to play it.

The flop

1 Take a wide stance at address, open the clubface a fraction, pointing it at the target, and aim your feet, hips, and shoulders to the left. The clubface should point directly at the pin, your weight should be split evenly, and the ball should be forward, just inside your left heel. Allow for a good amount of knee flex.

2 Make a full backswing, allowing your weight to move naturally onto your right side at the top. Like when hitting a fade, swing the club along the line of your body and not along the ball-to-target line.

3 If you commit to the shot, the club will arrive at the ball on a shallow path traveling from outside to inside the ball-to-target line. Your weight should be split evenly at impact, as it was at address. This has the effect of adding loft to the club for a higher, softer flight.

Open the clubface at address, move the ball forward, and take a wide, athletic stance. Make a full swing, keeping the clubface pointing at the target for as long as possible through the ball.

SOFT HANDS

It is important to have "soft" hands when playing any short-game shot. However, this is particularly so for the flop shot. Having soft hands will create a "dead" flight that allows the ball to land extremely softly. Try this on the practice ground and you will see just how important this is.

4 **Swing through to a full finish. Feel as if the clubface is** pointing at the sky for as long as possible during the swing. This is the final key to creating a high trajectory, so, as you play this shot in competition, let this be your only swing thought.

Belly wedge and hybrid chip

A versatile short game will help you deal with any conditions or unique scenarios a golf course can throw at you. If you can develop the simple two shots on these pages you will become a more complete player. The belly wedge and hybrid chip are both easy to master but incredibly helpful in two difficult positions. Learn how to play them and do not be afraid to use both techniques while playing in competition.

Be creative

These shots were developed by top players as they practiced. Be creative as you practice and you may find an unusual solution to a certain scenario.

Belly wedge

1 Take your putting stance and grip at address, ensuring the ball sits forward in your stance. This enables you to strike it slightly on the up, making contact with the equator of the ball and finding a strong, top-spinning roll. Move your hands down the grip a fraction—this will also help you strike the equator of the ball.

2 Now make a normal putting stroke. The rhythm of the stroke should be as smooth as possible. Concentrate on keeping the wedge low through the stroke; a shallow angle of attack will help the leading edge to strike the middle of the ball.

When to play these shots

The belly wedge shot should be played when you find your ball resting against the collar of the rough surrounding the green. In this scenario, playing a chip is risky as there is no room for error to find a clean strike. This shot allows the leading edge of the wedge to strike the equator of the ball.

The hybrid chip is useful when your ball is sitting on a bare patch of grass just off the green. This shot, played like a putt, bumps the ball into the air (over any slightly longer grass between you and the green) before running out to the flag. For both shots, you should take a moment before you play to look at the undulations on and around the green.

THINK...

For a belly wedge, move your hands down the grip, set the ball forward in your stance, and make a smooth, low stroke. For a hybrid chip, move your hands down the grip, stand close to the ball, and make a smooth putting stroke.

Hybrid chip

1 Take your putting grip, move your hands down the shaft, and stand relatively close to the ball. Your posture will naturally become more upright. You will notice that the toe of the hybrid on the ground sits up a fraction.

2 Make a normal putting stroke. A small amount of hinge in your wrists is fine, but do not let too much creep in because this will only add unwanted loft to the shot. Accelerate gently through impact and let the club swing through to a natural finish position.

Above The belly wedge shot is a helpful alternative to a normal chip.

Checklist

Learning how to become a more versatile player should be fun. Use this checklist for a quick reminder about how to play five crucial shots.

Fade

Set the club at the target at address but aim your feet, hips, and shoulders left of your ball-to-target line. Your stance should seem open at address. Swing along the line of your body and you will cut across the ball through impact. Concentrate on keeping the clubface pointing at the target for a fraction longer through impact.

Draw

Point the clubface directly at your target and then set your stance closed to your ball-to-target line. Swing along the line of your body, ensuring that you make a full and powerful release through impact.

Trajectory control

To play a low punch, move the ball back in your stance and place a fraction more of your weight on your left side at address. Make a shorter, softer swing than usual to reduce the amount of backspin created at impact. To add loft to a shot, move the ball forward in your stance, allow more weight to sit on your right side, and make a full, aggressive swing.

Belly wedge

To play the belly wedge, move the ball forward in your stance and take your putting grip. Make a fluid putting stroke, using the leading edge of the wedge to strike the equator of the ball.

Hybrid chip

For a hybrid chip, again take your putting grip but stand a fraction closer to the ball. Make a fluid putting stroke and the ball should bump into the air before running out like a putt.

Fault fixer

No matter how much you practice and how long you take to ensure all the basic essentials are in place, bad shots will creep in. Identifying the problem and implementing a series of fixes are the quickest ways to get back on track. However, faults in the golf swing come in a range of different guises, which can make self-diagnosis somewhat difficult. The fixes in this chapter simplify this process.

Left Lay a club down, aiming at your target to help with alignment.

Opposite Simple errors will creep in. You need to know how to fix them.

Accuracy check

It is amazing how many bad shots can be traced back to simple errors at address. No matter how vigilant you are simple but avoidable errors will creep in to your alignment. To avoid this, head to the range to work on your alignment every few weeks.

Slice

Perhaps the most common fault in the game, a slice occurs when you cut across the ball with an open clubface. The ball shapes aggressively to the right, leaving you short and usually in score-killing trouble. The key to solving the problem is to change the path of your swing, driving the club from inside to outside the ball-to-target line. The drill opposite should help you stop cutting across the ball through impact and straighten out that slice.

Knowing your swing

Having a good coach will help you to understand your own swing. The more you know the easier the self-assessment will become when things go wrong. Study your swing with a coach and don't be afraid to make changes yourself when mistakes creep in.

THINK...

Swing the club from inside to outside the target line and ensure your weight is moving toward the target through impact.

Left If you understand how you swing the club, then faults will be easier to fix.

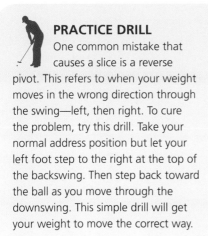

Right Use the headcover drill to improve your swing path.

Headcover drill

Place two headcovers on the ground around your ball at address, as shown here. The gap created between them illustrates exactly the path the club should take through the ball. If you slice, you are likely to hit the first and second headcovers as you cut across the ball. Swing back and through slowly, ensuring you miss both headcovers and you should start to follow the correct path.

SLICE

Hook

While the slice is the most common fault in the game, a hook is
one of the most destructive. In this instance, the ball flies viciously
left and usually only stops once it runs into trees, bushes, or long
grass. Stamping out the problem as soon as possible is essential.
The following tips and drills will help you straighten out your ball
flight, and keep the danger that lingers on the left side of the golf
course at bay.

Above Use two clubs to check your takeaway.

Above One-handed swings help synchronization.

Check your takeaway

A hook usually comes when you swing
through impact from too far on the inside,
closing the face as you make contact with
the ball. Take a good look at your address
position. Check that your grip is neutral
and that the clubface is not closed in
relation your feet. Lay two shafts on the
ground, on your ball-to-target line. The gap
between the shafts represents a good path
at the start of the takeaway.

Synch drill

To hit powerful, accurate shots, your arms
and body need to work together through
the swing. If you are struggling with a hook,
the chances are that your arms are working
faster than your body, closing the clubface
at impact. To rediscover the timing of your
move, simply make a series of one-handed
swings. This will give you a feel for how your
arms and body should work.

Above Move your left foot back at address.

Above It is also worth checking your grip. See pages 24–27 for more details.

Left foot back drill

Another drill designed to straighten out a faulty swing path is to hit a series of shots with your left foot back at address. Make a normal swing from here. The position of your body forces you to swing less from the inside on the way down. Hit 10 or 15 shots with your feet in this position and the ball flight will quickly straighten out.

Pushing and pulling

There are certain similarities between pushes and pulls and slices and hooks. The one crucial difference, however, is the angle of the clubface through impact. Like a slice, a push flies to the right of the target but without any sidespin. The flight may be straight but the direction is poor. A pull is the opposite—it flies straight left without hooking. Those who struggle to tame a slice will occasionally hit a pull, not a push. The same rule applies for those who hook.

What causes the push

If your bad shot is a hook, you will also suffer occasionally from hitting a push. Crucially, the path of the club through impact attacks the ball from too far inside the target line. Unlike a hook, however, when you hit a push, the clubface will be aiming straight right. This is the reason the ball heads right without any right-to-left sidespin.

Push cure

A push is sometimes the result of a swing that lacks conviction. If you try to guide the ball toward the target instead of powerfully driving through to a full finish, you risk leaving the clubface open. In this situation, you need to concentrate on your finish position. Make sure that you swing through to a full finish, so that your chest is facing the target and your weight is on the outside of your left foot.

Right In the finish position, your chest should be facing the target and your weight should be on your left foot.

BALL POSITION

Regardless of whether you are suffering with a push or a pull, check your ball position. If the ball is set too far back, you are likely to hit a push. If the ball is too far forward, a pull is likely. Make sure that with an iron in hand, the ball is sitting in the middle of your stance.

THINK...

"Hit out" on the shot if you suffer with a pull and make sure the ball is not too far forward at address. If you suffer with a slice, make sure the ball is in the middle of your stance and concentrate on swinging through to a full finish.

What causes the pull

Think about the swing path that is to blame for a slice. As the club cuts across the ball, moving from outside to inside the ball-to-target line, the ball flies left and spins to the right. If you struggle with a pull, the clubface will be pointing left at impact and you will lack the sidespin that causes the ball to fly right.

Pull cure

Whether you are suffering from a push or a pull, you will need to straighten out your swing path. Look at the headcover drill on page 133; this illustrates the ideal swing path and forces you to commit to this line through impact. If you start struggling with a pull out on the course, concentrate on sending the club to the right of the target as you drive through impact. By "hitting out" on the shot, you should be able to straighten up the swing path.

Right "Hit out" on the ball through impact to help improve your swing path.

PUSHING AND PULLING

Fat and thin strikes

Whereas hitting a slice or a hook can be disastrous for your score, there is perhaps nothing more frustrating than hitting a succession of fat or thin strikes. If your ball striking is letting you down, there are likely to be some unnecessary movements in your swing. The drills on this page will simplify your technique to ensure you make consistently sweet contacts. The good news is that mistakes here should be easily rectified.

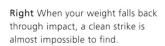

BALL POSITION

In the same way as for pushes and pulls, you should check your ball position. If the ball is too far back, a thin contact is likely. If it is too far forward, a fat contact is most likely. With an iron in hand, the ball should sit in the middle of your stance.

Reverse pivot

As explained in Lesson 3, a reverse pivot occurs when your weight moves in the wrong direction through the swing. If you are leaning back through the downswing, the club will "bottom out" too soon, either striking the ground before the ball (fat) or catching the ball on the upswing (thin).

Right When your weight falls back through impact, a clean strike is almost impossible to find.

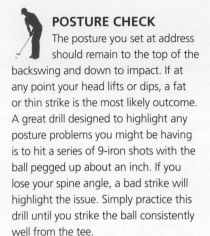

POSTURE CHECK

The posture you set at address should remain to the top of the backswing and down to impact. If at any point your head lifts or dips, a fat or thin strike is the most likely outcome. A great drill designed to highlight any posture problems you might be having is to hit a series of 9-iron shots with the ball pegged up about an inch. If you lose your spine angle, a bad strike will highlight the issue. Simply practice this drill until you strike the ball consistently well from the tee.

THINK...

Make sure that your head is not lifting or dipping during the backswing or downswing. Force your weight to move onto your left side through impact. Check your ball position.

Weight transfer drill

To force your weight onto your left side through impact, place something, such as a folded towel, under the outside of your right heel. At address, you will notice that your weight sits more on your left side than usual, but this is fine. Hit a series of shots and you will notice that this drill does a great job at preventing you from falling back through impact.

Right Force your weight onto your right side to guard against the reverse pivot.

Checklist

No matter what your handicap, the errors in this chapter are certain to creep into your game. Use this simple checklist to stamp them out.

Slice

Make sure that your setup position is square, so that the clubface is aiming at your target and your feet, hips, and shoulders are square to the ball-to-target line. Your grip should also be neutral. Stop yourself from cutting across the ball and instead, swing from inside to outside the ball-to-target line. Above all, do not start aiming left to limit the damage of your slice—this will only accentuate the problem.

Hook

Do not aim to the right of your target but set square angles at address and ensure that you are not attacking the ball from too far inside the ball-to-target line. Try hitting shots with your left foot set back a fraction at address to neutralize your swing path. Make some slow, deliberate one-handed swings to ensure that your arms and body work together throughout.

Push

Be extra careful to ensure that the clubface is pointing directly at your target at address. Use the same swing path drills to solve a slice to ensure the angle of attack through impact is not to blame. Check your ball position—any slight errors here can cause the ball to go straight right.

Pull

Use the swing path drills to check that you aren't making any simple mistakes. Swing through to a full finish, with your weight on your left side.

Fat and thin strikes

Make sure that when you hit with your irons, the ball sits in the middle of your stance. Check your spine angle—it should remain the same from address right through to impact. If you lift or dip your head, a poor strike is inevitable. Make sure that your weight is not on your back foot through the downswing but is instead moving toward the target.

How to practice

The time you spend working on your game is incredibly valuable. Unless you plan on taking up golf for a living, the chances are that your opportunities to practice will be limited. That's why you need to make sure that every practice ball you hit will help improve your performances. A structured, technically sound practice routine lies at the heart of reducing your handicap. In this lesson, we will look at the best ways of doing this. Through drills, games, and careful note-taking, the advice that follows will help you get the most from your valuable practice time.

Above Note down what you are working on and how you are doing it.

Take your time

Never rush through your practice routine. After you hit each shot take a moment to think about what just happened and how the swing felt. By slowing yourself down, you'll be able to take stock and even make some notes in your book. You should also run through your preshot routine in practice. This might seem somewhat excessive, but as the pressure mounts on the course this will help you find a positive, confident mind-set.

Start by stretching

Whether you are preparing for a teetime in an hour or simply to hit 50 practice balls, always start with a few simple stretching routines. By swinging two clubs slowly at the same time, you will soon loosen up. Alternatively, perform the kind of upper and lower body stretches you would use before playing other, faster, sports. You need to make sure that from the first practice ball to the last, you are loose and capable of making a free-flowing swing.

Practice games

An effective practice routine will work to improve certain key fundamental techniques while preparing you for the challenge of the course. The drills and games featured here are designed to develop the basics and establish them under pressure. Practice games are a great way to improve your game—they keep your interest going and with an element of competition will create crucial pressure.

Above Hit pitch shots to five different targets to improve distance control.

Pitching game
A natural feel for distance control is essential when you are pitching. You can develop this in practice by taking on a series of simple challenges. Pick five targets on the range between 50 and 100 yards away from you. These can be yardage markers, flags, or any other easily identifiable object. The aim of this game is to hit consecutive shots to within around 10 feet of each target. By changing the target for each shot, you will need to rely on your natural feel for distance to succeed. Add an element of pressure to this game by going back to the start every time you miss. You only complete the game once you've hit all five targets consecutively.

> **THINK...**
> Head to the range with a friend, and create pressure by setting yourself tough challenges that develop key fundamental techniques.

Shot-shaping game

A great way to practice, regardless of what you are working on, is to do it with a friend. Having another person there to keep an eye on your technique can be extremely helpful. With two of you there, any games can become competitions. A great one to try is this: Take it in turns to play shots, trying to find a different shape or flight for each ball you play. For instance, you would set up to the ball and your partner would say, "high fade." You would then both have an attempt at producing this shot. Whoever hits the best shot in each round gets to choose the shape and flight for the next round, and so on.

Above Practice with a friend to create an element of competition.

Left Hit a series of shots with different clubs along the same line.

Line drill

To score well on the course you need to be able to hit every club in your bag well. This drill tests your ball striking under pressure— from wedge through to driver. First, pick a large target on the range—this can be a green, a yardage marker, or even a building in the distance. Starting with your most lofted wedge, hit one ball with each club in the bag. The task here is simple: Hit each ball in line with your target, ensuring each shot goes farther than the last as you move up through the clubs in your bag. Only finish the game once you have successfully hit all 13 shots in a line with each ball going farther than the last. As you move into the longer clubs, pressure will start to mount and you'll need to rely on good fundamentals and a committed swing.

Chipping practice

A good short game requires a fine balance of touch and technique. When you practice, make sure that you use drills that will train both aspects. If you become too technical—reliant on setting good positions—you'll lose your feel for the pace of the greens. These drills are designed to create a solid technique while also promoting a free-flowing swing that optimizes your feel.

Above Get your weight moving by walking to the target.

Above Bowl a ball to illustrate the weight shift.

Walk-to-target drill

If your short game lacks feel, it could be because your chipping stroke is too mechanical. This drill instills a good fundamental technique while ensuring that there is still a fluidity about your stroke. Hit a series of shots, but as you strike the ball, start to walk toward your target. Your upper body and the sole of your wedge should both be aiming at the target as you walk. Think of the position that a pitcher or bowler gets into when they release the ball—your finish position should resemble this. This simple drill creates a smooth chipping action and forces you to release your upper body toward the target.

Below Keep the club moving low through impact with the under-the-shaft drill.

Under-the-shaft drill

If there are two of you practicing, this drill is an excellent way to develop a key aspect to the technique. A shallow swing will help you use the bounce of the club when you chip. Get a friend to hold a shaft out, about a foot closer to the target than the ball. The idea is to pop the ball up over the shaft but keep the clubhead working underneath it. This is an excellent way to highlight how the club should work through the ball. It also proves just how effective the loft is in getting the ball airborne.

CHIPPING PRACTICE

Putting practice

A good practice putting routine should be enjoyable. It should not feel like a chore to stand on the green working on your game. After 60 minutes of well-structured work your scoring potential will vastly improve. These drills and advice explain the best way to use your valuable practice time, so you walk away with an improved technique as well as a deft touch.

Above The down-the-channel game will help improve your distance control.

Down-the-channel game

Good long-range putting is about having a natural feel for the pace of the greens. This drill will test your instinctive touch. Create a channel on the green using the shafts of your other clubs, as shown. The channel should be around 12 yards in length. Now the aim of this challenge is to see how many balls you can leave in the channel. It sounds simple enough but each ball you hit has to go farther than the last. Make a note of how you fare and then try this game later in the season—you'll be able to judge your improvement.

> ### THINK...
> Develop your feel for long-range putting, and when you are faced with a breaking putt concentrate on the apex. Work on your technique to ensure the stroke comes from a simple rocking of the shoulders.

SHAFT-UNDER-ARMS DRILL

A solid putting stroke is created by a simple rocking of the shoulders. Your hands should remain passive through the stroke because they keep the putter head working on-line. Place a shaft under both armpits and make a series of practice strokes.

Check how the shaft moves. If it isn't working up and down on a straight line, you are employing an unnecessary movement that could throw the putter head off target. Work on this aspect of your technique for 10 minutes every month and your stroke will become extremely solid.

Shift your focus

When you are faced with a breaking putt, your focus should shift from the hole to the apex of the curve. If you are concerned about the hole, you'll miss the break and the ball will have no chance of going in. In practice, find a putt that breaks sharply and stick a tee peg in the ground adjacent to the apex of the curve. Now simply aim to narrowly miss the tee and your success rate will improve drastically. Remember when you get to the course to think about breaking putts in the same way.

On course

Now that you have hopefully established all the keys to a solid game, it's time to test yourself in competition. This is where all the time you have spent practicing will pay off, rewarding you with impressive scores. It is important that when you head to the course you are thinking about building a score and not the technique. Be confident in the fact that you have practiced well and let your natural feel for the game take over. If you can do this, while remaining calm under pressure, your handicap will soon head in the right direction.

Stroke indexes

You will notice that the tee markers on every hole detail the yardage, hole number, and also the stroke index. The stroke index is a way of ranking each hole on the course in terms of its difficulty, with 1 usually being the hardest and 18 the easiest. When you play in a Stableford competition, the stroke indexes will tell you where your shots come. For instance, a 14-handicapper will get a shot on holes ranked 1 to 14. Likewise, if you are playing a match and receive four shots from your opponent, these come on the holes ranked one to four. Use the stroke indexes to help you formulate a plan for each hole. If you are playing stroke index one, play it safe. Keep the ball in play at all costs, knowing that a bogey will not be a bad score. Conversely, be relatively aggressive on the holes with a higher stroke index because these are where the majority of your birdie chances will lie.

Building a score

Playing 18 holes in a competition is a roller-coaster. You'll have good scores and bad, good luck and bad, so try not to get caught up in one particular moment. This can be incredibly hard, but remember that one bad hole does not necessarily have to lead to a bad overall score. Stay calm and focused throughout; you never know where your next birdie will come.

Opposite Stay in the present and think about one shot at a time.

Below Use the stroke index to help create a strategy.

Strategy

Knowing when to attack and when to defend are crucial. For any one golf shot, there is usually a range of different factors to keep in mind, from the direction of the wind to where all the danger lies. The more you play, the quicker you will calculate these factors. Here is what to look out for and how to react to certain common situations. Avoid hitting your shot before you've mapped out what you expect to happen carefully.

THINK...

Take time to consider the direction and strength of the wind because even only a light breeze can have a big influence on your shot. Acknowledge the trouble and come up with a strategy that will help you avoid it. Never follow a bad shot with a bad decision.

Wind direction

Rarely will you play golf in still, calm conditions. Even a light breeze can have an effect on the flight of the ball, so you should always think about the direction of the wind before you play any shot. There are a couple of ways of doing this. The first is to throw up some grass and look to see where it flies. Alternatively, if the wind is hard to judge, look at the top of the trees that surround you. These will offer invaluable clues as to what the ball will do once it reaches the top of its flight.

Above Throw some grass up in the air to get a feel for the wind direction.

Where does the trouble lie?

Whether you are on the tee or the fairway, you should always look to see where the most dangerous trouble lies. Mind coaches will sometimes tell you to block this out but, as anyone who plays regular competitive golf knows, this is virtually impossible. Instead, acknowledge where the trouble lies and then pick a strategy to steer you away from the danger. A good tip to help you focus on where you do want the ball to go—and not where you don't—is to pick a small target in the distance. It can be a building or a tree, but it should be small. This will narrow your focus and help set a positive mental outlook before you play.

One simple rule

The one simple strategy-related rule that you should never forget is: "never follow a bad shot with a bad decision." This means that if you have hit your ball into trouble, your next shot should be to get you back to safety. By taking on a tough recovery or aiming at the flag from thick rough, your chances of making a disastrous score will rapidly increase. Be sensible—if you hit a bad shot, try to limit the damage by getting your ball back in play as soon as possible.

Above See the trouble and come up with a strategy to avoid it.

Above Never follow a bad shot with a bad decision and know when to play safe.

Match play tactics

Match play is a very different game to stroke play. There are certain tactics to employ in match play that you do not need to worry about when you are trying to build a score in a normal stroke play competition. These will deflect pressure onto your opponent and away from yourself. You should not feel bad about using them— match play is all about pressurizing your opponent. Here's what to do in certain key match play situations.

Giving putts

In match play, you are allowed to give your opponent a putt. For example, if we are in a match together and your ball comes to rest a couple of inches away from the hole, I can give you that putt, which means that you do not have to knock it in. A good tactic is to give your opponent quite long putts (around 4 feet) early on in the round. This will not only demonstrate your generosity—which may well be reciprocated—but also, more importantly, it will prevent your opponent from getting their eye in from this crucial range. As the pressure grows toward the end of the round, do not give them the same 4-foot putt. Suddenly, they will need to make the putt under pressure, not having done so earlier in the round.

Left Give short putts at the start of the round but not as pressure mounts at the end.

Left Use the honor to your advantage by hitting the fairway.

Four-ball tactics

One of the most enjoyable formats in golf is to play in a four-ball better-ball match play (two teams of two play each other and the two best individual scores on each hole go against each other). In a four-ball match, the team, instead of the individual, has the honor. This can be helpful on the green. If your playing partner has a 6-foot putt for par and you have a 20-foot putt for birdie, your partner can play first. If they hole, you will have the freedom to be aggressive with your putt, knowing that the team already has a par in the bag.

The honor

In match play, the honor is a valuable commodity. If you play first and hit a great shot, your opponent will feel huge pressure and may also be forced to change tactics. Some of the world's best players will try to ensure that their tee shot does not travel as far as their opponent's on a par 4 or par 5. This means that, as they are farther from the hole, they will have the opportunity to play first to the green. Hit a good shot in this scenario and the other player will be forced to hit a similar shot under much greater pressure.

DON'T GIVE HOLES AWAY

One of the most frustrating things you can do in match play is to let your opponent win a hole with a bad score. You should always try to force your opponent to win holes with pars at least. If this means finding the fairway with a 3-wood and not taking a risk with the driver, then so be it. If you can keep the pressure up throughout the round, your opponent will know that if they make any simple errors, they will be handing you the hole.

THINK...

Give your opponent short putts early in the round but make him or her play them at the end. Where possible, try to capitalize on having the honor and not to give holes away by making simple, strategic mistakes.

Coping with pressure

The more competitive golf you play and the lower your handicap becomes, the more pressure you will face. Coping with nervous tension is a huge part of the game and is often what separates the truly great players from the talented ball strikers. Keeping your nerves under control requires calm thinking and an innate trust in the technique you have worked hard to develop. Here's what to do when the pressure mounts—and a good score hangs in the balance.

On page 90, we explained the importance of a preshot routine as you putt, but this also applies with the long game. Develop a simple, repeatable routine and when the pressure mounts you can switch to autopilot and rely on the key movements that have proved successful in the past. Here is a simple and effective preshot routine.

Preshot routine

1 **Stand behind the ball and pick a target in the distance.** The target should be as small as possible because this gives you a greater margin for error. This also helps you set a positive mental outlook.

2 **Place the club behind the ball before setting your stance.** Be careful to ensure that it is aiming directly at your target—any small mistakes here can have disastrous repercussions.

CHECK YOUR GRIP PRESSURE

When the pressure mounts, it is a natural reaction to try to exert control by strengthening your grip. Strangling the grip is a telltale sign of pressure and causes a jerky movement that lacks fluidity. Keep your grip pressure light and you will be able to make a normal swing, even under extreme pressure.

THINK...

Use a preshot routine to help you stay calm under pressure. Make sure that you are not strangling the club and play to your strengths.

3 Now set your stance. Make sure that your ball position is good and that your feet, hips, and shoulders are parallel to your ball-to-target line. You are now in a great position, ready to make a good swing. If you can repeat this simple sequence for every shot you hit, you'll be in a strong position to cope with pressure.

Above Commit to the shot and trust your technique.

COPING WITH PRESSURE

Index

rotation 46–9, 58
slice 132–3, 140
takeaway 42–3, 58, 134
transition 52–3, 55, 59
weight transfer 50–1, 55
wrist hinge 44–5, 58

T
takeaway 42–3, 58, 134
target line 31
tee markers 150
teeing grounds 8
thin strikes 36, 138–9, 141
trajectory control 122–3, 129
transition, swing 52–3, 59

U
unplayable lies 12
uphill lies 112–13

V
Vardon grip 26

W
water hazards 8, 13
wedges 14, 17, 60
    belly wedges 126–7, 129
    greenside bunkers 105
weight distribution 33, 69
weight transfer 50–1, 55
winds 93, 122, 152
woods 14, 16
wrist hinge 44–5, 58
wrists, flicking 74

Y
yardage markers, fairway 67

Picture acknowledgments

Special photography: © **Octopus Publishing Group**/ Richard Neall. **Other photography**: **Alamy**/Denkou Images 13 top. **Fotolia**/Secret Side used throughout the book. **Getty Images**/Jack Hollingsworth 145 top; /Mike Powell 19. **istockphoto.com**/ David Anderson used throughout the book. **Octopus Publishing Group**/ Steve Bardens 13 bottom center, 18, 83, 85 right, 91, 92 left, 92 right, 93 top, 93 bottom, 97 right, 154; /Angus Murray 2, 4, 7, 9, 10, 11, 15 top, 20, 23, 25 top, 31, 33 bottom, 35 right, 41, 43 top, 45 bottom, 47, 51 top, 53, 57 bottom, 61, 63 top, 64, 67 bottom, 69 bottom, 73 top, 75 top, 79 top, 89 bottom, 99, 101, 102 left, 102 right, 103 left, 103 right, 105 bottom, 107 top, 109 right, 110 left, 110 center, 110 right, 111 top, 111 bottom, 115 top left, 115 top right, 117 left, 119, 121, 123 right, 125 right, 127 right, 130, 131, 135 right, 143, 144, 145 bottom, 150, 151, 152, 153 left, 153 right, 155, 157 bottom right; /Mark Newcombe 79 bottom.

Executive Editor: Trevor Davies
Managing Editor: Clare Churly
Executive Art Editor: Penny Stock
Designer: Ashley Western
Photographers: Simon Jollands and Richard Neall
Picture Library Manager: Jennifer Veall
Production Manager: David Hearn